WHO MESSED WITH MY LIFE

By
Beverly J. Beach

PublishAmerica
Baltimore

First printing

ISBN: 1-4137-7320-6
PUBLISHED BY PUBLISHAMERICA, LLLP
www.publishamerica.com
Baltimore

Printed in the United States of America

Dedicated to Aunt Kate:

She's in her seventies now and her health isn't good, but her blue eyes still have a sparkle in them. You know a wisecrack could erupt any time you feel like you're in the presence of love. When Aunt Kate is near, you get such an urge to hug her and to say "I love you." The children at family reunions all run to Aunt Kate for their hug and kisses before they run off to their day of excitement and adventure. Need a pan of baked beans, ask Kate. Need a 25 pound ham baked, ask Kate. Going on a trip, ask Kate. She has a bag packed at all times on "red alert." Jellies, jams and pumpkin bread are given to family and friends as Christmas presents. She never forgets a birthday. The card is always right on time. She has had many head winds in her life and has stood firm. We know it's safe to believe in Aunt Kate. She has given a piece of herself to each of us. I treasure mine. Aunt Kate is my Irish Leprechaun.

Aunt Kate is my blessing.

Acknowledgment

My colleague, John Cull, has been a wonderful source of encouragement, support, suggestions, critiquing, and downright bossy sometimes, but always, always, with my best interests in mind. This writing process, with all its hard work and its disappointments, would be so much more difficult if John Cull wasn't in my corner. Thank you, John.

PROLOGUE

The Good Book says, "The poor will always be among us." I also believe abused and neglected children will always be among us. To think otherwise is living with your head in the sand.

The foster child system came into being to help abused and neglected children have a chance at a better life. And an imperfect system it is.

I know both sides of the foster child coin as I spent thirteen years in three different foster homes. Ages five to eighteen. At two separate times, as an adult, I was a foster parent.

Unless you have been a foster child, you do not have any idea what damage such an experience does to a child's emotions. When you leave the foster child system everything isn't miraculously healed. The effect follows you into adulthood.

In the following words I will present a child's journey through the seeming solution to my father's neglect of myself and of my younger sister. My mother was out of the picture by the time I was three and a half.

I am not interested in pointing a finger at the participants of this journey as some of the people involved are still living. I have no desire for revenge in any form. I will use fictitious first names for parties involved in the second and third foster homes.

I am writing this book to help people learn the true havoc that is wreaked on children's lives while in the care of the foster child system. Lives caused by circumstances beyond their control, with no knowledge of how to protect themselves from the consequences of decisions made by others, or have an advocate to stop negative, life-altering behavior. Our emotions are up for grabs. Who has the strongest position, wins? That isn't the foster child. They are the victims in this scenario.

THE EARLIEST YEARS

"Mommy, where are you going?"

I asked my mother that question when I was three years old, standing between two sets of railroad tracks. My younger sister and I were there because our mother took one of our little hands and led us up a grassy slope which led to those tracks, not very far from the house we were living in. When she had placed us between the tracks, she dropped our hands and walked back to the house. This is the first memory I have of my life.

I remember looking to my right to see if that big, black, noisy thing was coming. I knew nothing about death, but I knew that big, black, noisy thing scared me. I wanted to get away from there before it came. My sister had just gotten so she could walk fairly well, but I wasn't sure I could help her over the tracks. And I felt, what I now know was panic. I recall, and again now know, what was a sense of relief when she was able, with my help, to get over the first track. I knew we would be able to get home. I remember feeling happy and safe.

Next, I remember my sister and I walking through the door of the house and seeing a very wide-eyed, open-mouthed mother staring at us.

My only other early memory of my mother was one evening she asked me if I had gone to the bathroom that day. I don't remember her exact words, but it had to do with a bowel movement. I told her I had, as it was the truth. She laid a towel on a table and another woman that was there grabbed me and laid me on my back, on the towel. My mother took off my panties, stuck something in my bottom, holding a can in the air and my tummy began to hurt. Both women were laughing the entire time. I cried. What hurt most was that my mother hadn't believed me.

* * *

My next memory is of my sister, father and myself living at a farm house. Evidently, my father signed on as a hired farm hand with room and board for him and his daughters as part of his pay. The wife of the farmer was to watch us while our father was working.

One night, it was raining hard and as dark outside as it could get. I was in the living room playing on the wide plank flooring with a horse-drawn milk delivery wagon toy. They must not have had electricity as there were lit lamps in the living room and kitchen. The farmer was sitting in a chair and his wife was in the kitchen which was right off the living room. I heard their two teenage sons come into the kitchen from outdoors. They were mad. My father was supposed to have done his chores. He hadn't. He wasn't even there.

One of the boys was going to put on my father's boots and I ran into the kitchen and told him he couldn't wear them, they were my father's. About that time, my father came into the kitchen and told me it was all right. My father had a soft voice and a kind look in his eyes. He turned around and went back out into the rain to do his chores.

Shortly after, we moved to another farm. This farmhouse was nice looking and the barns were in good shape, too. I have four memories from our time spent there.

We had a bad ice storm one night and when I looked out my bedroom window the next morning, everything was covered with a thick sheet of ice. I could see a car in the ditch a short distance down the road. I saw my father coming out of the barn. He had hitched up a pair of big work horses and was holding the reins, walking behind them. I figured he was going to pull the car out of the ditch. The horses would slip on the ice, regain their balance and slip again. He was afraid they might break a leg, so they were put back in the barn.

* * *

Another memory was of the Fourth of July. A lot of children and adults were sitting, standing or running around the front lawn. Someone asked me if I wanted a sparkler.

I said, "No."

My sister took one. I believe my refusal came from the fact my father wasn't there. I was sure they didn't want him there and that upset me. Everyone lit their sparkler when it got dark and I wish I hadn't said no, as they were having such a good time. I didn't dare ask for one, and went into the house and up to our bedroom.

There was a fair sized barn between the house and the main barn where huge blocks of ice were stored. They cut these chunks of ice in the winter from a nearby lake, selling them to people with ice boxes. Sawdust was put between each layer. Why, I don't know, but it sure stuck allover me as I climbed to the top row.

I hadn't told anyone what I was going to do because I didn't know what I was going to do when I got outdoors. It wasn't until someone "found me" that I knew anyone was looking for me. I was told never to go into that barn again.

There was a small house down the road a little way on the other side of the road. The lady of the farmhouse walked with my sister and I to that house one day for a visit. Had no idea why. She went back to the farmhouse. The lady we were visiting was very nice. I got a motherly feeling from her. I liked her. I didn't know who she was.

One day, I went over there by myself. It didn't enter my mind to tell anyone. It wasn't being bratty,, it just didn't enter my mind that I should tell someone. The farm lady was really angry at me. I sensed she looked down on this other woman. She wasn't dressed extra nice and the house was small and plain. I found out years later, the lady was my Aunt Kate. Later, she became the closest to a mother I had.

We left that farm and moved to another one on the top of Foots Hill just outside of Odessa, New York. There was a big house and a big barn, but not kept up as well as the last place. There were horses, cows, sheep and chickens. My sister, father and I shared a room.

Three memories from there:

The farmer's wife, daughter (I think it was a daughter), my sister and I went to the village of Odessa.

I don't remember what we did there, but we picked up a puppy and I held it on the ride home. I kept making the puppy yelp and the farmer's wife kept telling me to stop doing that. I kept on and she said when we got home I was going to get a spanking. We got out of the car and the farmer's wife went into the house.

In my mind, I thought if she didn't spank me right when we got home like she said, I figured she COULDN'T spank me now and told my sister so. She evidently told the woman because she came out of the house and spanked me. I think that was my first lesson in "splitting hairs." It wasn't the last time my sister deliberately caused me trouble.

Another memory was when the women of the house were waiting on my father to come home, so he could take over watching his daughters. I heard someone say he was probably drunk again. I didn't know what drunk was, but I told them I didn't believe them. He had told me he was going to the doctors. He wouldn't lie to me. I cried and someone took me to the doctor's office, so I could see for myself. I opened the door and looked around the waiting room and didn't see him.

I was so disappointed. I felt he didn't love me. When he came home, I asked him about it and he said he had been sitting behind the open door ... that's why I didn't see him. I believed him.

I don't believe it now.

Then the event happened that totally changed my sister's and my life—causing me one of the greatest hurts I have ever known. I was five years old.

One evening, I overheard the farmer's wife telling someone that we were going the next day to a place called the "court-house." My sister and I would be taken away from our father. I went into our dark room. I couldn't ask my father about it because he wasn't there. I fell asleep waiting for him. He wasn't home the next morning.

The next day, my sister and I were dressed in pretty dresses and we were taken to the Schulyer County Courthouse. I saw my father standing outside in front of big wooden doors that were in a big, red building. I ran down the sidewalk, put my arms around his leg, begging him not to let 'them' take us away from him.

I don't recall what he said to me, but I had a feeling of assurance he wouldn't let 'them.' We would all be together, for sure. My father was a fairly short man of slight build. I adored him.

My sister and I were taken into the building and sat on a long, long seat. There were people sitting on each side of us. I saw my father come into the room and sit down up front. Different people would stand up in front of a man who wore a long black dress. Then our father stood up and I heard that man tell my father that my sister and I were to be taken away from him.

I screamed and screamed, and cried, and went into hysterics. Whoever was with us would not let us go to our father, even to say goodbye. They pulled me screaming and kicking down the hallway and outside to a car that was parked alongside the building. The back door of the car was opened and we were told to get inside. The door closed.

We were alone with strangers. I was angry and scared. The lady who was sitting up front in the car turned around and offered my sister some candy that was in a paper bag. My sister took a couple pieces. She offered me some candy and I told her, "Keep your ole candy."

The man who sat up front started the car and we drove away to our new home— in a strange area and in the opposite direction from where we had been living. The man died three weeks after we moved into their home. I worried what would happen to my sister and me, now. Then, as if I had pulled a switch, I stopped thinking and feeling. This would happen to me many times over the following years.

Foster Home #1

My sister and I lived with Mother Collum four years. She told us to call her that. I had been anxious about what to call her. I wanted something to be sure about.

Any problems I had while living there were pretty much my own doing. Such as, it was one Christmas season and a large package had been dropped off at the house by the rural delivery mailman. We were alone for awhile which was unusual. I told my sister, being the package was addressed to us, we had a right to open it.

She wasn't in complete agreement with me. I talked her into it. We carried the package to the basement and tore off the outside paper and then opened the box. There were coloring books, books that had pictures with certain spaces not filled in.

You had to look on another page to find what went there to punch it out, lick it, and stick it where we thought it belonged. There was a lot of stuff in the box.

When Mother Collum got home, we were roller skating on the concrete basement floor.

She was upset! Those were our Christmas presents from our maternal grandparents. I didn't even know I had any.

I finally admitted it had been my idea because my sister was going to be punished, too. I had to eat supper upstairs on the wide landing at the head of the stairs. It wasn't the last time, either.

* * *

I didn't like to go outside in the winter, so when Mother Collum would tell us to get our winter outer-wear on, I would pretend I couldn't hear her. She always made me go out. I would sneak out a book, find the side of the house where the sun was shining, sit on the ground next to the house and read until I figured I had been out long enough to satisfy her.

We had to walk a mile and a half to the country school we went to—so in the winter, Mother Collum made us wear long john bottoms and heavy cotton thigh-high stockings. The stockings were held up with a piece of elastic that had the ends sewn together.

In the spring when it began to get warm, I would roll my stockings down and my long johns up as soon as we got out of sight. I would reverse the process on my way home from school.

One day, I rolled my stockings up but had forgotten to roll down my long johns. When I walked into the house the look on Mother Collum's face told me I was in trouble, but I didn't know why.

She soon told me.

One of the long john legs had worked its way down over my stocking. I wasn't aware of it. My sister got to take her long johns and stockings off the next day. I had to wear mine another week. I learned a lesson on that one. I also had to eat supper by myself, upstairs.

There were never more than fourteen kids in the one-room schoolhouse—all grades combined. The older kids were at the back of the school and the youngest were up front. There was a coal and wood burning stove used for heat in the winter. Each family took turns bringing food that could be heated on the stove, so we could have a warm meal at lunchtime.

* * *

It was another Christmas season and for art we were given a twelve-inch square of ecru colored muslin by the teacher. A picture of Santa from the waist up, holding a candle and holder in his gloved hand, had been traced onto the material. We were told to color the picture using crayons. I colored mine pink and yellow. That upset the teacher and she gave me another piece of cloth, telling me to color it correctly. I colored it pink and yellow. I liked those colors and thought it was mine and I should be able to color it the way I wanted to. I know she was upset again but I can't remember what happened.

At school, when the weather was good, we would go outdoors for recess. We played team games. There was a creek at the edge of the school property and one day, during recess, I was absorbed looking for crawdads and tadpoles. Eventually, I realized I didn't hear any noise and looked around.

No one was there and I knew recess was over. I hadn't heard the bell ring. I was scared to go into the school because I thought the teacher would yell at me, and I was also scared not to go in. I went in. Nothing was said and I sat down at my desk.

* * *

One winter night, there had been a bad ice storm. Mother Collum drove my sister and I to school that day, very slowly. We got out of the car, but we couldn't stand upright as we tried to cross the highway because of the ice.

We got down on our hands and knees, pushed our metal lunch boxes across the highway, and crawled on our hands and knees right up to the school steps. The teacher stood on the top step, holding out a broom for us to grab on to so we could get inside. I remember thinking it was wrong and dangerous to go out on a day like that. But, I admired the teacher for being there early to get a fire going, and helping us to get inside. She was a tall, rather heavy set woman— plain looking—and she became my heroine.

* * *

One summer, I kept begging for us to sleep outdoors. Mother Collum finally agreed.

We took sheets, so we could put one on the ground to lie on and one to put over us if we needed it during the night. It was a perfect night, warm and lots of stars. I was so excited, but that was before I realized the ground was so hard.

I kept moving around, sideways, farther up or down the lawn, but I couldn't find a spot that would fit to my body. I began to wish I was in my comfortable bed, but knew better than say anything as this whole thing had been my idea. It was beginning to get daylight when I finally went to sleep. I found out everyone else had a good night's sleep.

There always was a garden, and one day Mother Collum gave me a pail that had kerosene in it. She told me to knock grubs and beetles off the potato plants into the pail. When I finished, she came out and set the kerosene on fire. That horrified me to deliberately kill something. She told me it was the only way to keep them from coming back.

Slowly, I began to feel I belonged at Mother Collum's home. She was kind and she was always there. I was beginning to feel content and secure enough to be an imaginative, spunky, little girl. The following proves my point.

She told me one day that the man next door had told her we could take some apples from his orchard. The ones on the ground. I pulled our little red wagon to the orchard and began picking up apples. After awhile, the apples on the tree looked better.

I would pick the biggest, reddish, ones. I pulled a wagon-load of apples home. The telephone rang and after Mother Collum hung up, she told me it was the neighbor that had called. He was mad because I had taken so many apples. I, honestly, didn't remember being told I could get just so many. What happened about it, I don't recall. A blocking-out had begun.

The people who lived across the country road from us only lived there during the summer.

He was some big shot in a school system. It was a lovely house. When the new school system got new playground equipment, they got the old swing set and teeter- totter—which proved to be my undoing one time.

They had a daughter around my age and a son a little older. She had a one-room playhouse and he had a one-room log cabin. It was great fun playing over there.

One day, I was forbidden to go over there to play, probably had something to do with a chipmunk. I stood by the side of the road for a long time watching the girl next door and my sister swinging.

I wanted to go there so much that I danced in place, but I remembered Mother Collum's words. The next thing I knew, I was looking both ways and shot across the road. I, truly, had forgotten I wasn't to go there. And this is the TRUTH! Gone.

I was swinging high and jumping out of the swing to see how far away I could land. I casually looked to my right and saw Mother Collum crossing the road with a switch in her hand. Then I remembered I wasn't supposed to be there. I got off the swing and ran to the opposite side of the teeter-totter.

She came after me. I ran a couple laps around the teeter-totter with her right behind me. I realized she wasn't going to stop and thought I might as well get my whipping over with. She started on me, but I didn't cry ... not from stubbornness, but because it didn't hurt. I sensed she wasn't going to stop until I cried, so I pretended to cry. I ate supper upstairs by myself.

* * *

We used to take pennies to the railroad tracks that were about a half a mile away, laying them on the tracks to see how flat they were after a train ran over them. Someone said you couldn't use nickels because they were too big and they would make the train tip over.

Another time, two neighborhood boys and two girls asked me to walk to the railroad tracks with them. I was so excited because someone chose ME to do something with them, even if it was laying pennies on the railroad tracks. Only that wasn't the reason.

Just before the tracks, on the right side of the road there was a very, very deep ditch. They told me they were going down there and I was to be a look-out to let them know if anyone was coming. I asked what they were going to do and received a vague answer.

I stood guard on the dirt country road, watching, and slowly began to wonder why. We didn't know much about each other's anatomies then—just the basics—and I thought on this and then thought about smoking. Both were wrong, I thought, and wanted no part of it. I went home.

That evening, I was outdoors and they came over ... mad at me because I had left. Someone had discovered them. I told them whatever they were doing was wrong and I wouldn't help people do wrong things.

* * *

One night, there was a horrible noise. It scared me and I put the pillow over my head. The next morning, I asked Mother Collum what it was. She told me it was a screech owl—that it meant someone was going to die. The next day, the neighbor did. That put terror in my heart every time I heard one after that. I counted noses the next morning, including the neighbors.

* * *

There was a small room off an upstairs bedroom where black walnuts were stored. They were from a tree on our property. Later, after the outer shell had dried, we took off the outer shell. Our hands looked like there was iodine on them. Then, we cracked the nut and picked out the nut meat, saving it for fudge and other stuff.

Every Sunday, Mother Collum drove us to Sunday school and when she couldn't do it the minister would pick us up. We stayed for church, also.

On Memorial Day, the Sunday school classes walked to the nearby cemetery to place small flags on the veterans' grave sites. I sincerely believe this early introduction in faith, subconsciously, got me through the following years. That is one Social Services RULE I agree with.

I was well on my way to having a normal childhood. I was beginning to believe someone did care about me. Love me, I wasn't sure of. I had no doubt that we would always live with Mother Collum.

* * *

The four years we were with Mother Collum, our biological mother never came to see us. She never sent a birthday, or Christmas card, or gifts for any occasion.

Our father did.

He didn't have a car and would have to hitchhike to see my sister and I. He never missed an important day in our lives. He was supposed to come this one day and didn't show up. No phone call. I was heartsick, sure he had stopped loving me.

This pattern has followed me through my entire life.

The next morning, there he was at the door. There had been a fierce thunderstorm the day before and a bridge over a waterfall that he had to cross had been washed away. Rather then turn back and go to where he lived, he spent the night under a pine tree for cover from the rain.

The road crew had built a footbridge over the falls and he continued walking to our house. He was soaked clean through and Mother Collum gave him some of her husbands clothes to wear. When it was time for him to leave, Mother Collum drove him back to the waterfalls and I waved to him until I couldn't see him anymore.

One day, she told us our father had asked her to marry him. I was so excited! My father would be living with us.

Then, she said, she had turned him down because she was aware the only reason he asked was so he could be with his daughters on a permanent basis.

Another hope, dream, gone.

She told us that he had asked the woman who owned the house he roomed at to marry him. She said yes. Then she said no. Then my father committed suicide. I was seven.

I overheard Mother Collum tell a woman friend of hers she didn't know if she would take us to our fathers funeral. I remember thinking she had better take us. If she didn't, I'd find some way to get there.

I felt a rage at not being allowed to have a say about something so important to me—again (like when we were taken away from our father).

The funeral was at the Methodist Church in Odessa, New York—four miles from the foster home I would be living in next. There were quite a few people at the funeral.

"Those are his children," whispered voices said as we walked up the sidewalk to the church entrance. We went in and stood by our father's casket.

I can still see the reddish, purple mark around his neck. I felt so void of feelings. We sat in a pew with Mother Collum and after a couple minutes my sister said she was going back to our fathers casket for another look. I grabbed her arm, pulling her down to the seat and said, "One look is enough."

Her reason appeared to be from curiosity, not love, and I thought it was the wrong reason for her to do it. Our father's death was just the beginning of heartache to come.

Mother Collum, shortly after, received a letter from Social Services stating she was too old to have foster children in her home any longer. They were going to remove us from her home and place us in another foster home. A date and time this was to happen was included.

I was on the brink of destruction.

* * *

The day Social Services was to come, Mother Collum got us up just as it was getting daylight. She had us get dressed, eat breakfast, and we left in the car.

I came back to life.

They weren't going to get us. We arrived back home after

dark. For three weeks, she didn't hear anything from Social Services and I let myself believe we were going to stay with her. I had such a sense of relief.

I was wrong.

She received another letter stating the date they were coming for us and if we weren't there, she would be arrested. She had no choice. I knew she didn't.

Mother Collum had gotten us a canary and a reddish color Cocker Spaniel. The dog's name was Prince. I loved him with all my child's heart. The woman of the house where we were going said we could bring the bird, but not the dog.

Something else I loved was being taken away from me. I couldn't face losing Mother Collum or Prince. I deliberately shut down. I mentally and emotionally left the world.

I wanted to die. I did die, inside. I have no memory of what happened after Mother Collum gave us this news ... Who came for us, the drive to the new foster home, or what happened when we got there. My sister was with me, this I knew.

FOSTER HOME # 2

The next foster home was located in the hamlet of Alpine, New York. I was nine. Any happiness I had, any sense of belonging somewhere or to someone, stopped when I moved from Mother Collum's.

I have NO good memories from the four years I lived in that home.

They had five children and only two lived at home—an older son in high school and a daughter, probably five or six. She had her own bedroom and it was filled with toys. I was in awe of it and wished I could have a bedroom of my own.

My sister and I shared a room. The daughter and my sister got along really well. I figured it was because they were so close to the same age. After awhile, I thought the daughter was spoiled.

In a month, the canary was dead. I didn't believe in goodness anymore. The mother wouldn't let me feed it. Said she would.

My sister didn't seem to be a part of my life. She was like a shadow. She had naturally curly hair and dimples. I had short hair cut straight around, at the middle of my ears. She was quiet and cuddly. I was neither. We were both blondes.

I was a tow-head blond. I had taken on the responsibility of my sister as we stood between those two sets of railroad tracks.

There was a large room where the lady of the house had her sewing machine and there was also a huge regulation pool table in the center of the room. There were hardwood floors and one spot was very worn.

I was running around the table, barefoot, and a splinter went into my right heel. I showed the lady where it went in. A piece had broken off. She did nothing but tell me to put my socks on. They were navy blue socks.

My heel kept getting more and more tender. It got so I couldn't put my weight on my heel. I would walk on the toe of my shoe. I would tell her how much it hurt and she would say there was nothing wrong with it.

One day she gave me ultimatum that the next day I was to walk on my heel or she would force my heel down. I knew if she did the pain would be unbearable.

That night, I was sitting on my bed looking at my heel when I noticed red streaks going up my ankle. This meant nothing to me. My sister was sitting on her bed and I told her no one would believe my heel hurt so much. So, later that night I was going to run away.

I would take her with me because she was my sister and I wouldn't leave her behind. I kept gently pressing on my heel and all of a sudden the other half of the sliver shot out along with a lot of pus. The splinter had probably been an inch long.

I felt so relieved then. She would have to believe what I had been saying right along. I was sure she would say she was sorry for not believing me.

I called to her to show her the proof. She came, looked at it, said nothing, and left the room. She never cleaned it, bandaged it or anything. It showed me how little she cared for me.

I felt worthless, totally worthless. My sister evidently told what I had said about running away. I got a harsh tongue lashing over it. I couldn't understand why my sister betrayed me.

* * *

One day, in the middle of winter, I was sent outdoors with a basket of wet laundry to hang the clothes on the clothesline. My fingers got so cold and the clothes were frozen stiff when I took them out of the basket, making hanging them difficult. My fingers began to hurt and I couldn't stand it so I went into the house, taking the basket of clothes with me.

I just wanted to warm my hands and thought maybe the clothes would thaw out some, making it easier to hang. I was hoping I could come in and get back outdoors without her knowing it.

She came into the kitchen, saw me, and asked why I was in the house. I showed her my hands. She told me to get back outdoors and not to come back in until I had every piece of clothes hung up.

I went back outdoors. I blocked out my anger. I accepted what I was told to do. The tears froze on my face.

There was company coming one evening and the lady told me to get the maple syrup from the pantry. I took the lid off and the top of the syrup was covered with a gross looking scum—and I said, out loud, that it looked rotten. She must have come and stood behind me because she told me I wasn't to say such a word in that house. I was surprised by her anger over such a thing. Any good feelings I had about company coming left.

The man of the house was a fireman at night, on a train coming out of Sayre, Pennsylvania, a rural letter carrier during the day, and bookkeeper for the M & M Club in Montour Falls, New York. He always seemed to be in the background.

One summer day, while everyone else was at their cottage on Seneca Lake, I had to go with the man on his mail route. He needed to get done early for some reason.

It was a beautiful day—sunny and warm. I saw beautiful butterflies, yellow buttercups, and sweet peas growing on a rusted fence and a bluebird. The man gave me a quarter. I was so excited! After we got back to the house and before we left for the cottage, I walked to the little grocery store at the other end of town and bought five cents worth of candy.

When the lady of the house found out I had spent five cents on candy, she yelled at me for being so wasteful. I should save my money. To me, I earned it, it was mine and I could do what I wanted with it, and I had only spent five cents out of a quarter. By the time she was done yelling at me, the enjoyment of eating the candy was gone. Dejection pierced me.

Another time when everyone was at the lake, I was at their house in the backyard, scraping the paint off a large wooden inboard motor boat that the man had bought. He was delivering the mail. I wondered why I was the only one who had to do these things.

Their oldest daughter and her family lived across the road. They had chickens. Eventually, they got rid of the chickens and I was told to clean out the chicken coop only it was as large as a one story house.

I was told I would be paid for doing it and figured because of the size of the building I would probably get five dollars. I did an excellent job. It took me five days to scrape the chicken manure from the roosts, the floor and to wheelbarrow it outside.

I was proud of the good job I had done. I was sure they would be proud of me, too. They gave me a dollar fifty. I was disappointed and hurt that they placed so little value on me. I didn't dare show it because I was sure they would take the money back. Right then, I made a conscious decision that I would never treat people that way. People were important and should be treated with respect, no matter who they are.

* * *

Every Christmas since their youngest daughter was born, the neighbors had her come over to their house on Christmas morning to get gifts that Santa had left at their house for her. When it was being talked about the first year we were there, I was sure my sister and I would not be included. I was astonished when on Christmas morning we were told to go to the neighbors house along with their daughter.

The feeling of being included as a family member felt good. The neighbors never did it again, not even for the daughter. The sense of worthlessness was piling higher and higher and was really taking a hold of my life and emotions.

The lady of the house had pleurisy one spring and was laying on the living room sofa for six weeks. I did the house work and if she didn't think I had done it good enough, I had to do it again. My sister and her daughter played.

I felt such anger I wanted to hit her and keep on hitting her. I wanted to hit everyone. I kept it all inside because I was being threatened that if I didn't behave, I would be sent to an orphanage or a reform school with each place being graphically described to me. I would be separated from my sister and I was all she had.

It scared the hell out of me.

My Aunt Kate, her children, and her father Patrick, lived just a few houses down and across the road. The lady of the house wouldn't let my sister or I visit them because they weren't the "best" type of people to be with.

Aunt Kate was Mother Earth. Her children and I rode the same school bus, but they were strangers to me. One day, they got on the bus and they were crying.

I didn't dare ask them why. I heard them telling someone their uncle (and mine) had been killed in an automobile accident. He was my uncle, but I couldn't join in their grief because I didn't know him. It was the first I had ever heard him mentioned. My uncle had died and I had no feelings about it except of isolation—from family and of feelings. I rode stoned-faced all the way to school.

The clothes I wore to school were the lady of the house old clothes. I called the shoes I wore "granny shoes" as they were black, laced up the front and had big, wide heels. She drew my hair back and put it in two braids. I was made fun of and called names by the children in the area where I lived and at school.

We went to a family get-together at Christmas one year at the home in Sayre, Pennsylvania, a brother of the man of the house. I overheard the lady of the house saying to her husband, 'I suppose we have to take them with us.' Later, she told me I was to keep quiet so I wouldn't embarrass them. I wandered around the house, finally sitting down. No one spoke to me or acknowledged me in any way.

One day, the lady of the house told my sister and I that our mother was coming to see us, on a weekend, for a visit. I hadn't seen or heard from her since the day she gave me the enema. I wanted to see her, yet I didn't.

It was more a sense of curiosity, I believe. She came with her husband and two children. I remember thinking they are my brother and sister and having no sense of the fact. We sat in the backyard and the foster parents stayed with us.

My mother was there for about half an hour.

She didn't give my sister or I a hug and a kiss when she arrived or when she left. Never saw or heard from her again until I was grown and made the effort to get in touch with her. I wanted a mother. Everyone wants a mother's love.

* * *

I did get to go ice skating on the creek behind their oldest daughter's house. The kids in the area came to skate there because it was a wide spot in the creek. I couldn't skate very well. I had weak ankles.

One time when I was skating, my skate hit a small branch that was frozen into the ice. I fell, landing full-force on my chin. The married daughter was skating with us and she looked over at me, but didn't come to where I was.

I sat up, dazed, holding my mitten to my chin. When I took the mitten away it was covered with blood. I skate-walked to the daughter. She took a look at my chin and told me to go home and get it taken care of, then skated away. My chin was bleeding so much I didn't dare to take the time to remove my skates. When I got to the house, I removed them before going into the house.

I showed my chin to the lady and she said there wasn't anything at the house to take care of it with, and that I would have to walk to the little grocery store for bandages. I still have a scar.

Their son, who was eighteen or nineteen, had a muskrat trap line along the creek in the winter. I had to go with him to check and see if he had caught anything. I, always, silently prayed he wouldn't. I was the only one that had to go with him. I didn't want to.

I was taken to the home of the Commissioner of Child Welfare to stay a week as the foster mother thought I had mental problems because I played by myself all the time.

I was to spend seven days there for personal observation. I had a bedroom all to myself. Their children were grown and gone. During the day I poked around in a large woodpile that was by the house. I was looking for different kind of insects and bugs. They interested me.

31

I was brought back to the foster home in five days. After the Freedom of Information Act was passed, I wrote to the county requesting to see my records and I read the reason why I was taken to his home. His analysis being that it was amazing that I was so well adjusted for all that I had been through. He wrote that I was a good girl. I knew when I was back at the foster home in five days, rather than seven, that I had passed a test. It gave me a sense of satisfaction that her plan hadn't worked.

* * *

The foster parents built a bare necessity cottage on Seneca Lake. They wanted a larger beach front so the adult males in the family would go out into the lake and bring in the large stones, lining them in a row as to how far out they wanted the beach to extend.

The plan was for us three younger children to go into the lake, pick up the rest of the stones on the lake bed, and throw them in between the big stones and the beach that was already there—to fill it up until no water showed.

Their daughter and my sister spent very little time doing it. I was out there every day it didn't rain, from morning until late afternoon. It never entered my mind not to do it. It also kept me away from her.

When that was finished, the next step was to take two little children's pails and go further down the beach and bring loose gravel, and dump it where we had thrown the smaller stones. It took me one whole summer.

When that job was done, I was given the job of pick-axing a clay bank under the cottage to make a place where the inboard motor boat could be stored for the winter. It was extremely difficult for me to do.

I was twelve. I kept at it all summer, though, I didn't make much progress. The adult males would work on it some. I don't recall if it got done that summer. I had become a non-thinking robot.

They had a canoe. I got to use it once. Their younger daughter and I were in it, with me being in front. She complained to her mother that I would get her wet when I paddled. I was never allowed in the canoe again.

I didn't do it on purpose. I knew better. Again my enthusiasm was cut off.

One last happening—I was sent to another daughter of theirs to stay for a long weekend.

Her husband was a musician. The living quarters was attached to a square dance hall. He played in the band and they were caretakers of the dance hall. I remember they had two small children and I was to watch them while the music and dancers were in full swing on Friday and Saturday nights.

I didn't know the daughter or her husband. I was eleven years old.

I went out into the dance hall Saturday night after the children had gone to sleep, reasoning that I would keep going back into the living quarters to check on them. Their parents didn't object to my being in the hall.

I stood on the sidelines. After awhile I was told it was time for me to go to bed. I didn't want to because the music sounded so good and I could feel, see, and hear the happiness in the room. I was having a hard time getting to sleep because I was so excited.

It was still going on when the husband came into the bedroom and tried to hug and kiss me. I pushed and pushed at him and started to cry. He finally said that he was sorry and left. I didn't dare go to sleep then.

At first, I didn't tell anyone—but then I told my foster mother because I thought something should be done about him and that an adult should do it. She talked to her daughter, she talked to her husband, he denied it and I was called a trouble maker. Another nail in my emotional coffin.

NO, I have not one good memory from the four years I spent in that foster home.

The foster mother decided she didn't want to be a foster parent any longer. My sister and I were sent to another foster home. Tossed away, again.

FOSTER HOME # 3

This foster mother's husband passed away suddenly, leaving her with children to raise. The youngest was six, the next was thirteen, and the oldest was fourteen—two boys and one girl.

Her husband had no insurance. They had a house. She chose to be a foster parent rather than go to work in a factory, this way she could be home with her children. Foster parents receive a check each month to help with expenses of caring for extra children.

The first week we were in her home, she had me, my sister and her daughter come into the living room for a discussion. It concerned menstruation and intercourse.

I was so embarrassed. I could feel that my face was very hot. When I was in the previous foster home, a classmate asked me if I had started to menstruate yet. I told her, no. I had no idea what she was talking about and asked the foster mother when I got home. She got mad, yelling at me never to say that word again. It was a good that this lady did because in a week, I was.

I lived there five years and at that time, I graduated from high school. Life wasn't any better there.

Her oldest son, who was a couple months older than I, would wake me, my sister, and another foster girl who slept in the same room with my sister and I, by having his hands under the covers groping us.

I kept grabbing his hands to keep him from touching me. After awhile, he would give up on me and go on to the other girls. We did not callout for help because we knew his mother would never believe us.

Believe me this, when I tell you, none of us, wanted to go through whatever fallout that would come our way.

He brought up at the supper table one evening that my sister and the other foster girl were whores, and his sister and I weren't but had a wish to be.

I found that to be extremely embarrassing, humiliating, and unfounded. Where I was concerned, his sexual harassment continued. I don't know if it did with the others. We never discussed it.

* * *

The summer between my junior and senior year in high school was spent working at a concession building at the top of the Watkins Glen Gorge in Watkins Glen, New York. My duties, as explained to me by my caseworker, was to baby sit the owner's two-year-old daughter.

My duties turned out to be much more. I waited on customers who wanted to buy souvenirs, cooked hamburgers and hot dogs, made sundaes, milk shakes, and swept the wooden floors after closing, putting a green mixture on the floor to keep the dust down the next day.

I stayed at the owner's house, being picked up my caseworker on Tuesday, late afternoon, and taken to the foster home so I could do the laundry. Which was a chore because there wasn't running water. I was returned to where I worked late Wednesday afternoon. This was the routine until a day before school started.

The foster mother and I seemed to get a little closer in our relationship and I remember thinking maybe I'm going to have a mother after all. One Tuesday, when I came home, she showed me a note her daughter had left on the buffet saying she thought her mother liked me better than her.

I, so much, wanted a mother but realized it wasn't going to happen.

A very bad time in my life was ahead. The oldest son offered to take me back to my job on Wednesdays. His mother thought that showed such thoughtfulness on his part. It would save a busy caseworker the trip. I would be filled with anxiety at the thought of being alone with him for a half hour drive that always took about twenty more minutes.

He would turn off onto a back country road, pullover to the edge of the road, and proceed to put his hands on my body. I struggled with him, grabbing at his hands, his arms, pushed at his shoulders, his chest to keep him away from me.

After awhile he would tire of the effort and finish driving me to the intended destination. One time, the routine started again and I was fighting him and felt emotionally drained. I started to cry body-wracking sobs, begging him, to please, please leave me alone

I kept saying please, please, please leave me alone, continuing to cry out my despair. He finally leaned away from me and said in a low voice that he would never do this again. He didn't, but it was weeks before I felt any amount of ease being in the car with him. My guard was always up, though.

It seemed after about five weeks of his driving me that something else came up that he had to do. A peace descended on me.

* * *

While I worked at the concession building, every time there was a change of movies at the local theater, I would walk along the top of the gorge, which was called the Indian Trail, down to the village of Watkins Glen to see the new release—and then I would walk up the winding road back to the house.

It was dark and too dangerous to walk back up the Indian Trail. The trail was little over a mile long, the road was three miles to the house.

There was only one night that almost put an end to my movie going excursions. I was scared on the way home and I mean really scared!! I could see car lights coming up the hill and terror penetrated me. I don't know why.

I looked for some place to hide, but the bank beside the road was to high for me to climb before the vehicle reached where I was. I literally threw myself to the bottom of the ditch, praying to God they wouldn't see me. They went on by, but I climbed the bank, hiding in the weeds. It was quite some time before I thought it safe enough to continue on home. I had a key to the house as they were all asleep when I got there. I was sixteen.

I didn't earn a lot of money, but saved $198.00. It was enough to pay for my senior class trip to New York City.

Five of us wanted to go to Washington D.C., but were out-voted. After the trip, I had three dollars left. Our class ring cost $12. I accepted the fact I wouldn't be able to have a class ring.

I didn't let myself care. The post mistress in Alpine gave me three dollars toward it and my caseworker loaned me the six dollars. There was a stipulation involved. I had to pay it back. I understood it as a lesson in responsibility. I paid her back, three dollars at a time.

The foster mother told me the only way I could go on the senior trip was if I were to share a room with her daughter, who was in my graduating class. The daughter had already signed up to share a room with another girl. I had hoped to have a few days away from her.

I didn't have a choice if I wanted to go, and I did, so I talked to our senior advisor and she arranged it. The reason the foster mother wanted me to share the room was because her daughter's boyfriend was a classmate and would be on the trip. The others girl's boyfriend was also a classmate.

One night, our class had been invited to a nearby hotel where another local school was staying. I went. The four of them didn't. When we got back to our hotel everyone went to their room.

When I got to my room and knocked on the door, no one answered. I could hear voices speaking low in the room. They wouldn't let me in.

I heard that hotels had house detectives and was concerned one would catch me standing in the hallway. I heard a noise and looked to my left, and saw a lone man walk across an adjoining hall. and I figured it was the detective.

I looked for a place to hide, saw a door, opened it, and went in. It was a janitor's supply room. I heard the door open and then close. After not hearing anything for sometime, I left the room and proceeded to knock on the door again, telling them a detective had been on that floor and to let me in.

It must have shook them up because someone opened the door and let me in. I was told to sleep on the floor by the door as there was no bed space for me. Someone gave me a pillow.

I could only sleep a few moments at a time. I remember being told to move so the boys could leave. I don't remember what went on in the room that night as I had learned to shut down my senses leaving me in a vacuum. I also didn't want to know because what I didn't know I didn't have to report to the foster mother.

I would have been the loser in any ensuing confrontation that would have surely have occurred. I prayed, literally, that no one else told the foster mother that her daughter and boyfriend had spent the evening and far into the morning in a room together. I lived in dread that she would find out. I would really be in trouble for not telling. A no-win situation.

One morning, the class was to go on a sightseeing tour. One of the sights was the statue of Liberty. I was so excited about having the opportunity to see it. I asked the girls to wake me if I wasn't awake in time to get ready to go. When I woke up it was very quiet in the room. The girls were gone.

There was no way I could make the connections to go even if I had known where the meeting place was located. I cried hard and for a long time. I felt I must be despised by everyone. I have no memory what I did the rest of the day or when the girls got back. Another place we were to go was the Bronx Zoo and I made sure I got to go there. The weekend in the city only added to my life's tapestry of being worthless.

High schools back then had the junior prom, senior ball, and the senior high yearbook. When the foster mother's daughter and I were in our junior year, she was chosen as one of the students to work on it.

When we were seniors, our class advisor, who was our English teacher, held a meeting in the class room to select candidates to work on our yearbook. I was one of five who were nominated to be in charge of the art work. We were called back into the class room where it was announced I had been selected.

I was stunned by the fact my classmates had chosen me. It was the high point of my life. I remember thinking that my foster mother would be happy for me. We lived four miles from the school, therefore, we had to ride the school bus. The daughter didn't ride the bus that day as her boyfriend had his own car, or possibly his father's car, and he got to use it on occasions. The car was in the driveway when I got home.

I opened the front door and heard loud voices coming from the kitchen. As I got closer, I heard the three of them saying I shouldn't have been chosen to be the art director. The daughter had done it last year and was the one who should have been chosen because of her experience. I was crushed emotionally. Why couldn't they be happy for me?

I slowly walked back to the front door, opening it as though I had just come in and closing it loudly to make sure they heard it shut. I didn't want them to think I was spying on them. Again, I blocked out the hurt, but the next day I went to see our class advisor and told her I thought the person who was art director last year should be the one to do it this year, also.

It was only right.

She asked me if I had been told to say this to her and I assured her I hadn't. She explained that my peers had chosen me and that was how it was going to be. I believed she called my foster mother because she said to me when I got home from school how my peers had chosen me and she was glad for me. I felt a moment of triumph and of equality, and stored it in my mind ... so I could bring the moment to surface and relive the feeling, when needed.

* * *

One December, when I was fifteen, myself and three others came down with polio. My sister, the other foster girl, and the foster mother's youngest child. We were affected by it, but not drastically so.

My sister's left eye was paralyzed, but with exercise it would eventually be all right. She wouldn't exercise it. The other foster girl was in bed for quite awhile. The feeling was she was faking it and her son didn't seem to be too affected by it.

It was discovered I had a slight curvature of the spine. I had to wear a steel-staved, heavy corset, which laced up the front, for

41

a year. I had to wear it all the time, except when I was in bed. No matter how straight I sat at school, the two one-inch wide steel bars would stick out from my back— pushing my clothes away from my body.

The boy who sat behind me would reach over his desk and pull on them. I sat there mortified. I ignored him, hoping that no reaction would take the fun out of it for him, plus the fact I was afraid to make a scene.

There I sat, ashamed of my own timidity. I realized it wouldn't stop until I did something. I turned around and asked him to stop. He didn't. The next time he pulled on the staves, I turned around in my chair, with a raised fist, and told him if he did that one more time I would hit him. Humiliation can give you false courage at times.

I heard him "psst" the boy who sat across the aisle from me and ask him if he wanted to change seats. The boy told him, no, he didn't want to get beat up. The bully never pulled on the staves again.

Confrontations always left me with silent, internal, tumultuous emotions that threatened my stability. How dare I defend myself. Who did I think I was. Now, the world would crush my very existence.

Since that one time, I haven't entertained the idea of running away. Then I wanted to, but I knew I would be found and my life would be more miserable, and I had no place to go. Every decision had to be made entirely by me as there was no one I could go to for help.

When I was fifteen and lying in bed one night, with the moon shining on my face, I looked up and asked God to take my life that night. I couldn't take my own life because it was against God's teachings, but he could make that decision.

He didn't.

The next morning, when I woke up, I reasoned to myself that I only had one more year left in the foster child system and then my life would belong to me.

I would be free. I could make it until then.

One hot summer day, the foster mother made me go outside in my bra—no blouse. I told her I didn't want to do that, it wasn't the nice thing to do. She said that it was just like a halter and to get outside.

I had to fight to keep the tears behind my eyes, shut off reality, and step outside. I was shaking with shame. I walked toward a bench that had a back on it and squatted down behind it. Her oldest son and a buddy of his were nearby. I was petrified they would come to where I was hiding and taunt me. If they did, I don't remember it or how long I was there or how I got to go inside.

* * *

When I had polio, I, also, had rheumatic fever and was in bed for three months. The day came when the doctor said I could get up. I was very weak from being in bed that long. I felt very shaky when I stood up.

The day the doctor told me I could get up, the foster mother had me ironing starched white shirts that her son and his friend wore. There were 21 shirts. After I had ironed about half, I felt that I was going to faint. I was sure she would let me stop and sit down. She didn't. She brought me a stool to sit on and told me to keep ironing. I did.

A series of things were happening, such as someone used chalk all over a door screen, and was taking oranges from the refrigerator—such type of doings. One evening, at the supper table my sister said she had sores on her tongue and the foster mother said she had been telling lies.

That night, the foster mother told me my sister had told her, 'I don't know why Beverly is doing all these things.' After the "tongue" episode, she confessed she had been the one to do them. I asked the foster mother why she would say that about me. She didn't know.

The house didn't have running water so we had to heat water when we did laundry or bathed. When the daughter wanted to bathe, she would tell me to bring a basin of hot water to her bedroom. When she was finished I had to go to her bedroom, get the basin of dirty water and empty it. I felt like a servant. .

Mother Collum came to visit my sister and I once. I was ecstatic to see her. She gave me a small drawstring beaded purse. It disappeared. It was the only thing I had that she had given me. I didn't question as to where it was. I was afraid as to who took it.

All I know was the daughter said how much she liked it.

The foster mother made it clear she didn't like Mother Collum coming to visit us. The foster mother told me that Mother Collum had been found wandering the streets of Elmira, New York, in a daze.

She and her husband never had any children of their own. My sister and I were all that she had. I wanted to visit her and hug her and tell her I loved her. I knew there was no use in asking. I blame Social Services for what happened to Mother Collum. If we had been left in her home, it wouldn't have happened. I was very angry.

* * *

Where I live now is a rural area. I take a lot of walks.

My husband and I went to the last foster home for a visit so

I could show off my baby boy. As we were leaving, my former foster mother informed me that she had gotten in touch with my biological mother to inquire about adopting my sister. She said my mother agreed to it.

The former foster mother said she couldn't afford to adopt two children. I was stunned. It was clear she had never intended to adopt me. By that time, I just accepted whatever happened. No emotion involved.

While I was still living in that foster home, one afternoon, the foster mother was gone. My sister, the other foster girl and myself were in our bedroom talking about nothing in particular. I heard the daughter holler my name from the bottom of the stairs and I answered her.

I knew better than not to answer. I heard her racing up the stairs and she burst into our room, screaming at me that when she called me I was to answer. I told her, calmly, I had. She continued to scream at me that I did not answer her.

I said to ask the other girls if I answered her but she kept ranting. I knew the girls were too scared to stand up for me. My mind exploded and the next thing I was aware of was my fingers around her throat—and I was squeezing, hard. The realization of my actions stopped me cold. I let go and stepped away from her. I knew I was in more trouble than I had ever been in my life.

I was sitting at the sewing machine, in the dining room, when the foster mother got home. I heard a whispering, she went into the enclosed front porch where a little wood and coal stove was and came back, standing behind me. I braced myself, but had no idea what happened— would happen—until I felt a blow hit my shoulder.

I knew I was in for a beating, and I put my arms around the side and back of my head. I had heard if you get hit at a certain place on your head that you could die. I was being hit with a piece

45

of two- by-four about two or three feet long. It went on quite some time, then I was ordered to my bedroom. I was not asked my side of the dispute, just hit. I have no recollection of the following days.

On the first part of June of my senior year in high school, the foster mother told me, when I graduated I had to leave her home, immediately. It was a Social Services law. I did get to stay until my wedding day which was the next month.

As for my wedding day, my wedding dress was a two-piece eyelet outfit that I wore to my graduation. The foster mother did make it.

I baked my wedding cake, which was a 9x13 white cake, I made the sandwiches for the reception to be held at the foster home and I set the table. I did everything. My sister and the daughter were scouring the countryside, picking wild-flowers for the church. As my father was dead, a brother of his walked me down the aisle.

After the wedding ceremony we went to the house. Then, I moved. I have to admit that I felt my wedding day should have been made a little more special for me. Right or wrong, that is how I felt. It seemed like every other day.

I left the foster child system with no sense as to who I was as a person. I didn't think of myself as a person. I had disassociated myself from life. I had even mothered myself. I was a flat line ___ . This is how I started my married life.

ON MY OWN

My husband's name was Ollie. We were married eighteen years. He died at 43 of a heart attack. Five children were born to us—from the oldest: Don, Pam, Deb, Nancy, and Barb. Later, there were fourteen grandchildren and five great-grandchildren.

I have been married and divorced three times.

On July 18, 2004, I was 75 and though I have overcome much, some demons still plague me. I have put the past in its proper place in my life, accepting that is how my life played out. It could have gone many ways as anyone's life can, but I own this one. It played out as follows.

First, I have not talked against the children's father to them nor will I now to anyone else.

Ollie and I lived with a number of different people for awhile after we were married. We, finally, were able to rent a ground floor apartment for ourselves. We had our first child by then.

No one ever talked to me about child birth and it came as a very scary experience. I knew NOTHING. Not even the basics—'like where does this baby come out.'

I was laying on a table in the labor room and heard two nurses talking. They mentioned that the woman who had delivered before me did so when they had her use the bathroom, before she was wheeled into the delivery room. I was told that I was ready to go into the delivery room, but I was to go to the bathroom first. I told her I didn't need to go. She insisted. I insisted I didn't have to go. I finally told her it was because I was afraid I would have the baby in there. She assured me that was a rare happening and it wouldn't happen to me, so I went to the bathroom. I didn't know what was going to happen next. .

In the delivery room, the pain really intensified. I didn't know why I was hurting so much or how long it would last. I mean, I was ignorant of the whole process. I went into hysteria. I screamed and kept on screaming and a nurse slapped my face. I heard the doctor say something, then something covered my face.

When I woke up, I was groggy, then it all came back. I started to get upset all over again, but realized that I wasn't in the same room. Slowly, I moved my right hand to my stomach and cried tears of joy when the stomach I knew wasn't there. I heard a couple nurses discussing how badly I acted. Their take on the situation was I had been given too much, whatever, to calm me down. A nurse, seeing that I was awake, came to my bed and told me we had a son. I asked if my husband could come in and, shortly, he did. He didn't look any better than I did.

The furniture in our apartment consisted of a large, round, oak table and four straight back chairs. It was loaned to us by my brother-in-law and his wife. This was in the kitchen.

A double bed and a dresser, also, loaned to us by my brother-in-law and his wife. My in-laws bought themselves a refrigerator, giving us the ice box they had been using. The kind you had to buy a large chunk of ice for and they gave us a three burner kerosene stove to cook on. At one end was a glass jug, turned upside down, which was full of the kerosene. When I wanted to bake, I put a square metal box on top of two burners. There was a door on the front and absolutely no way to regulate the temperature.

We didn't have a washing machine, so I washed all our

clothes, towels and sheets in the two section kitchen sink. I used a scrub board and my knuckles would bleed. I would hang the clothes on an outside clothes line. In the winter, I hung the laundry on a folding wooden frame. After about three months of this, we purchased a wringer washing machine and I was so grateful.

I have a natural curiosity, so I went into the basement to see what it was like. I saw an old tan wicker settee and brought it upstairs. The landlady told my husband we could use it. It had a padded cloth covered seat and back. There was a design printed on the cloth, but it was faded. I took regular crayons and colored the design. I felt real pleased about it. I had done something to help our situation. Now I had living room furniture.

At a later date, my in-laws bought two upholstered rocking chairs for our living room. I don't remember how we got the crib for our son. When he was two, we bought a twin bed with a railing for him to sleep in. We needed the crib. Our second child had been born. A daughter.

I had never even held a baby before our son was born. I'd never been around babies and was unsure how to care for them, correctly. I bought a book (not Dr. Spock) but gleaned little practical advise. It was when I was reading the section where it stated if your child grew up to be a murderer, thief, or a person of such caliber, there would be signs, but they didn't list what they were. I dropped the book in the wastebasket. I remember thinking, I'll just have to love him through.

I was changing his diaper when a thought came. I still, clear as a bell, remember thinking, "I DON'T KNOW WHAT LOVE IS!" I realized it was true.

I let out an agonizing wail and dropped to my knees, holding my son's foot and cried the cry of complete desolation. My son's future was at state. A child needs love to grow into a mature, compassionate human being, otherwise, he is just going through the motions of living. It scared the hell out of me that was the kind of life I was going to give him.

I didn't know what to do. I entertained thoughts of leaving his father so he could find a good woman who would be able to give my son love.

I finished diapering him, held him, looking at his beautiful face so innocent and trusting, for a long time. I held him close to me and walked and walked that apartment. Finally, hysteria wore off and I pledged I would do the best I could. No one else was going to raise my son. I figured I'd use common sense. I had become more sure of my role as a mother by the time our oldest daughter was born.

* * *

I took pictures of my children as they were growing up. I had no pictures of my childhood and it left an empty hole in my life. I wasn't going to have empty spaces in my children's life.

I didn't realize it at the time, but I had decided my children were my life. No matter what circumstances I found myself in, no one, no one, was going to look down on them. Whether there was a man in the house or not, there was a lot of money or not (there wasn't), their lives would be lived on a 'value' level. They were important.

We didn't have a car, so Ollie had to hitchhike to work every day. We moved to an apartment in a nearby village which was where his job was located. Our third child was born while we were living there. A daughter.

A co-worker of Ollie's told him of a farmhouse that was available to rent eleven miles from the village. We needed a larger place to live and we had a car by then, so we rented it. It had eleven rooms, no running water and no central heat. You take what you can get. Rent was twenty-five dollars a month. We lived there nine years.

Our water came from a well on the property. The handle was the kind that turned in a circle. A large size chain would catch on metal prongs that stuck out from a metal disk. There were small rubber cups spaced around the chain and these were what brought the water up and out the spout.

We always had to make sure we had some water in the house during winter, so we could heat it and pour the water down the well to melt the top layer of ice that would form. Sometimes, I forgot and I would have to go outside, put snow in a bucket and heat that on the stove. We had a bottle gas cook stove.

Our heat came from what was called a space heater. It used coal as fuel. As long as coal was shoveled into the firebox we had heat. At night an extra amount of coal was put in, the damper adjusted, so the fire would last overnight. The ash would fall into a metal container at the bottom of the stove that had to be emptied regularly to provide air necessary for the coal to burn.

Once a week, a large metal tub would be placed behind the stove in the winter, so the kids had some heat around them as they sat in the tub. I would rotate each week as to who would be first to get their bath as the water wasn't dumped after each child had their bath. The bath water had to be heated on the cook stove. The rest of the week they got what I called, sponge baths.

No running water meant no inside bathroom. A pail with a lid, which was made specifically for the purpose, was used by the children and I emptied it each day. Actually, it was night as I didn't want people driving by to see me carrying it to the outside john. I wouldn't let my children do it as I felt it was degrading and my children were not going to be degraded.

When my oldest children were five, four and three, I became

aware they were not being disciplined and were acting unruly. I was waiting for Ollie to help in this area, but he wasn't much of a talker and I accepted the disciplining would be my responsibility. I was concerned that was how the children would remember me. It was.

My one daughter did tell me that was how she saw me as a child, but now is grateful because, as she said, 'I would have gotten in a lot of trouble. When I would start to think about doing something wrong the thought would come into my mind, if I do that mom will kill me.' That helped a little.

One of the younger daughters was forever acting up and I would spank her. I always talked to her afterward, telling her I cared for her and wanted her to grow up into a good person. That was why I spanked her. One time after a spanking I asked her why I had spanked her and she replied, "because you love me. I wish you didn't love me so much."

I had read somewhere that a wife should always look good for her husband or he might leave her. My hair was always combed, my dresses were always clean, starched and ironed. My only makeup was lipstick. I used a tube until I couldn't get anymore out of it.

I would go a couple months before I dared to ask if I could get a new tube of lipstick. I felt it was a luxury and I was being selfish to want one. I would, eventually, get up the nerve to ask. The answer was, yes.

A thought came to me that I couldn't be a good mother and remain the kind of person I was. My children would suffer for it and so would I. I hated feeling so worthless, but the thought of doing something about it terrified me. I wanted to be in the shadows, the background. I'll work hard but don't look at me, don't see me.

The church would be a good place to start my

transformation. Church people are supposed to love everyone. They aren't supposed to find fault and criticize you so it would be a safe place to start. The nursery, that's where I would begin. Babies can't find fault with you. It took every bit of courage I had to make the phone call to the minister and offer my services. He sounded surprised and told me that people just didn't call him and offer to help in the church.

I was given the nursery. The room was upstairs and had a large window that overlooked the sanctuary. I bought pink and white checked material and made lined curtains for the window. I made a train out of black material and hand stitched the pieces onto the curtain. I embroidered black smoke coming from the smokestack.

My sewing machine had a wooden box that would be set over the sewing machine head when it wasn't being used. It had a foot treadle and was made by White. That sewing machine got a real workout over the years. Store bought clothes cost so much.

I grabbed my courage with both hands and asked to be placed in the next step up. I was going to be teaching a Sunday school class. Of course, these were very little children. I enjoyed them.

I learned to make a diorama in a shoe box. I made a long scroll with the Ten Commandments printed on it in fancy lettering and I drew a fancy design. I hung it on the wall of the Sunday school room.

I was informed Children's Day was coming up and my class was to have a part in it. I worked with the children giving each child something to say in front of the congregation. The shy ones I would stand up with, holding their hand, if necessary. It was a case of the shy leading the shy. I closed out the fact there was anyone else in the sanctuary or I couldn't have done any of it.

When our part was over I sat on the pew with the children and marveled at myself. I had gotten up in front of people and spoke. It was a giant step for me and I cherished it because I knew I had a long, long way to go and wasn't sure I would be able to make it. I was so scared of life. Not having anyone for support and minus coping skills, it can be scary. What I think I had and didn't know was a faith in God.

* * *

Ollie and I talked about having foster children in our home and decided we would. I wanted to know some foster children had a good home where they were treated kindly. Treated as though they really were important. In the couple years we were foster parents, there were six different children placed with us.

Two of the girls were able to be reunited with their families before, too, long. One of the first children was a little boy about five. He was slow mentally and emotionally. A girl, around five, came on crutches as she had a hip condition that required her to wear a corset with an attached strap, with a hook onto the heel of her shoe. She was not to put any weight on that leg.

The case worker told me if she didn't stay off that foot her hip would be permanently damaged. You can imagine the fear I had when I would find her swinging with the foot loosened from the hook, or when I would check her during nap time to discover her jumping up and down on the bed. I felt so inadequate that I couldn't keep this from happening. I was told at a later time after she left our home there was no damage.

One tiny, black-haired girl we had would scream when it was bath time. She would go into hysterics. I reported this to her case worker and found out that where she had lived, previously, would put her in skin-burning hot water to take a bath and, even though she screamed, left her there. If I had been told that to begin with, I would have known how to handle the situation.

That really upset me that they hadn't.

We were contacted about taking a fifteen year old boy into our home for three days. He was deaf and couldn't talk. He communicated by writing. He was to be transferred to a new place that was being built on Long Island, especially, for children with his condition.

This was a totally new experience for us, but beings it was only three days, we said yes. The three days turned into weeks.

It was Easter Day and the young boy started writing to me that he had seen angels in his bedroom and that the Virgin Mary talked to him. I wasn't sure how to handle this, so I called his case worker.

She told me that he would be moved from our home in THREE days. Then, she proceeded to tell me that in the last home he lived, he would take their chickens by the head and swing them around and around until they died. Also, he had a sexual tendency for boys our son's age. In answer to my question, no, he could not be moved before. I had never heard of something like this and I didn't sleep one night while he remained in our home.

The case worker came the morning of the fourth day and drove him to a local state mental hospital. She called me the next day and related how the trip had gone. He kept pointing out angels in the sky all the way to the hospital and that she stopped and looked at everyone. When they were almost there, he reached from the back seat and pulled her wide-brimmed hat down over her face. She took off the hat. It had been an anxiety filled hour and a half.

Ollie and I made the decision to cease being foster parents. I was emotionally drained. I had no idea all this other stuff went with taking foster children into your home. I just wanted to make some kids feel safe and wanted. We weren't sure if this was good for our own children. It was a big disappointment for me.

Sometime in the ninth year of living at the farmhouse I began to tire of the hard work involved without the conventional conveniences. I hadn't said anything about it because I didn't dare. I felt I should be happy with what I had. There were people who had less.

One day, I was in the check-out line at the grocery store and standing in front of me was our former landlady. I wanted to say hello to her, but was afraid I would be rejected. She turned around, saw me, and told me the apartment we had before was available.

I told her it was too small now as we had more kids and furniture. Her kids had been after her to move into the smaller of the two apartments. If we would like the larger apartment, she would move. I asked what the rent was and she said $40 a month. I got so excited, inside. I told her I would have to talk to Ollie and we would call her either way we decided. I practically ran to the car.

I told Ollie about my encounter on the ride home. We both seemed to want to make the move, but then Ollie wasn't sure we could afford the raise in rent. Negatives began to be listed and I spoke up and said, "Let's not talk about it anymore. Let's just do it."

It was raining the night we moved. The apartment had three bedrooms, living room, dining room, kitchen, and full bath. I literally would stand in the bathroom doorway and stare at the toilet. Sometimes, I'd go over and flush it for the pure joy of it! And the tub, wow! For a long time the bathroom was my favorite room.

We set up everyone's bed the first thing after all the furniture was in the house. I also put up the curtains in the bedrooms. Then, the kids went to bed. Ollie, too, as he had to get up early to go to work.

When everyone got up the next morning the entire house was settled. Dishes in the cupboards, pots and pans in the cupboards, food in the cupboards, and I was cooking breakfast when they came into the kitchen. It was as though we had been living there for some time. I didn't want their lives disrupted anymore than necessary. To me, having to move again was trauma enough. In a year, we had owned our own home. I belonged somewhere.

HAMILTON STREET

The final piece of my dream puzzle was in place. I had my own home. A place where no one else lived that could cause me trouble and heartache. It was permanent. I could make plans. I, also, wanted our home to put my children on a level playing field with the majority of their friends and classmates. And a place they didn't have to be ashamed of as I always felt in my life.

It was a small house, but had three bedrooms, living room, dining room, kitchen, full bath, laundry room and full basement.

The living room and dining room had hardwood floors. I was in awe of them and took real good care of them. I put up white café curtains at all windows. Early American was the decor. There was a small front yard, side yard and back yard. The driveway was on the other side of the house. The house had forest green shingles as siding. I loved it.

Ollie said we could use a second income to help with our new expenses. I said I wouldn't go to work until our youngest child was in first grade. Getting kids started off right where school was concerned was of primary importance, I believed.

Just before she started kindergarten, I did fill out an application at a local business. I was sure they wouldn't hire me because I didn't have work references, but I could show Ollie I was trying.

They called me. I had the job. I agonized about it a few minutes, then told them I couldn't accept it because our youngest child was starting kindergarten that year and she needed me to be there when she came home from school. She needed someone to tell her daily news too. I told Ollie what had happened. He wasn't exactly pleased, but I told him I would go to work next year, for sure. I did and at the same place that called me the first time.

Not having parents that I could have some pride in, I was determined my children would be spared such feelings of shame. Again, I gathered all my courage and contacted the local Methodist Church to offer my services as a Sunday School teacher. I got fifth graders! There were only four or five kids to begin with, then more, slowly, came into the class. I did my best to make the class interesting. I followed protocol up to the point where it became boring.

For quite a few Sundays, we would meet in the classroom and leave from there to attend different churches in the area. Including, a Jewish synagogue. That was where I discovered the Salvation Army was a church.

Some of the parents agreed with what I was doing and helped by providing transportation. I felt strongly that observing how other churches worshiped, and that they all worshiped the same God, would help make them more tolerant of and accepting of other faiths, leading to peaceful coexistence, which to me was the Lord's plan for us.

We had gone to five churches with the Catholic church being next. I received a phone call at my home from my supervisor TELLING ME I was not to visit any more churches, to stick to the curriculum the church provided. I did, but I did it my way. I didn't want to lose the kids as I felt a strong faith in God is extremely important to their future as teenagers and on into their adult years.

I must have done something right as I was approached to be

on the Board of Commissions for the church, children's division. I accepted and was in charge of setting up Vacation Bible School, one year.

I left the board after a couple years as my feelings of insecurities around adults that I felt were smarter, and world wise, than me became overwhelming. I would have what I now know were panic attacks. Children, I can work with and accomplish things without the panic attacks.

I still thought I needed to be more important in my children's eyes and make them more proud of me, so I offered to be a Girl Scout leader. I knew nothing about girl scouts. I attended training sessions with my heart in my throat, but determined to succeed.

As in teaching Sunday school, I would block everything out of my mind except for my goal.

There was a woman who was leader of the senior girl troop and she was the ideal leader. Her troop had gone overseas to be part of worldwide programs. I called her all the time because I was so unsure as to how to start being a leader. She would tell me, however I wanted to, but I didn't understand. She had to be a saint to put up with my hysteria. I looked at the Girl Scout manual and picked out a badge I thought would be an easy one for the girls and easy for me to teach. Slowly, by observing other troops, I learned what the senior scout leader meant when she said, however I wanted.

The girls in my troop were fifth- and sixth-graders and the troop was under the title Junior Girl Scouts, later called Cadet's. The only way my girls could get a badge was to thoroughly earn it.

One of my daughters, in another troop, had a sash full of badges, but they weren't earned and that distressed me. There couldn't be a sense of accomplishment or pride in them.

Did I say something to the troop leader or our superior? No. It would have been easier for me to swallow Dráno than to speak up. I figured I would be the best leader I could, knowing my girls were learning, growing in character and compassion.

My troop grew to 43 girls and I was told it was too big a troop. I recruited an acquaintance of mine to be my assistant. I also formed a committee with another acquaintance to handle various aspects of our programs. She did an excellent job, very dependable and knowledgeable.

Four girls were appointed to be a patrol leader of each of our four patrols. I gave the girls responsibilities and allowed them to carry them out. They performed their duties in a professional manner. If, for some reason, a planned event was called off, I would contact the patrol leaders, informing them to call the girls in their patrol.

One such planned event was a hike in the woods. Programs were in place, outside people set up to teach about the things you find in a woods, someone to lead singing, someone to lead in games and we had just enough chaperones (an adult for ten girls).

During the previous week I received phone calls from some of the mothers who said something had come up and they couldn't chaperone after all. Three changed their minds. The By-Laws of the Girl Scout organization are very definite on the safety of the girls.

I contacted the patrol leaders and told them to call the girls in their patrol and let them know there would not be a hike and what the reason was for the cancellation. They were very upset and begged to be allowed to go. I couldn't say yes.

I wanted the parents to get the message that my troop wasn't a baby-sitting service, that the parents were an integral part and if they didn't participate, there would be no outside events for the girls. I knew the girls would take care of the problem within their own home. They did a good job because in a matter of days I had two mothers for every ten girls. I reset the date and didn't get one call of cancellation. Everyone had a great time, including the mothers.

There was a regional, day-long event set up on the Hobart College Campus in Geneva, New York. My troop was responsible for the closing ceremony. I was anxious about it and my quest for perfection took over. I didn't dare contact the senior scout leader who had been such a source of help to me and obsess about what to do and how to do it. I was literally sick to my stomach. It finally hit me that the girls were the ones to come up with a program, as part of their training to be leaders and we went with their plan.

It was fine—not perfect—but fine and the girls were so pleased with their efforts and for being trusted with such an important part of the program. They were a great group of girls.

While there, some of us took a tour of the college and felt like it was holy ground. The first woman to become a doctor attended this college.

I was a Girl Scout leader for four years. I worked on it every day, including the day of our meetings. It became too much and I gave my resignation.

My sister-in-law kept having miscarriages and this one time the doctor told her she was going to have to stay in bed the entire time of her pregnancy, so, for seven months I would go to their home once a week and clean house and do whatever else she needed done. Her husband was a great help to her doing laundry and such.

The last month she stayed with her mother who lived in Erie, PA. She wanted to be near her brother who was an osteopath. She trusted him and wanted him there for the birth. The baby was a little girl. The baby lived for three days. She moved back to her husband's home and her mother came, also. It devastated my sister-in-law and she wouldn't go out of the house or see anyone at their home.

This went on for a couple months and I decided to go to their home and see her, unannounced. As I was getting ready to go out the door the phone rang. It was her mother asking me to come over as this had been going on too long.

I got there and sat at the kitchen table with her mother. She told me her daughter was in the bedroom off the kitchen. After a few minutes, she came out and sat in an overstuffed chair by the bedroom door. I talked to both of them, just everyday stuff. She never said a word but I knew she was listening.

After about ten minutes, I saw tears forming in her eyes and she went back into the bedroom. I left shortly, not knowing if my visit helped the situation. It evidently did because her mother called a couple days later saying that a friend had come to visit and my sister-in-law talked to her, briefly.

When we lived in the country the only children my children had to play with were each other and that usually went well. The village was another thing. On Hamilton Street, our backyard butted onto someone else's backyard. Our children played together.

There were two boys the same ages as two of my girls. One day, my youngest child came into the house crying, saying the little boy who was her age, six, hit her with a stick. I explained to her to forget it because he probably wouldn't hit her again. He did.

She came in crying and this time I told her to ignore him and play with the other kids—that it was wrong for her to hit back. She came in again, crying, and I told her the next time he hit her she was to take the stick away from him and hit him with it, once.

sure that he would and that I would get a call from his
mother. He did. She did. Their boys weren't allowed to play with
my children anymore. I knew I couldn't count on that and I was
right as they were back in two days.

My third child was extremely shy and a boy at school kept
bothering her. She would get upset and instead of confronting
the boy she would go into her shell. She had a girlfriend and one
day after most of the kids had left school for the day, this boy
came up to her and started with his routine. She must have had
enough because she and her friend talked him into getting
inside her long hallway locker and they slammed the door shut.

The girls walked out of the school to his yells of protest. The
janitor let him out, later. No one knew who did it. He must not
have told anyone. Maybe, she put the fear of God in him. He
never bothered her again. She put the fear of God in him. She
also played first seat in the school orchestra.

One of my intentions in getting involved in church and Girl
Scouts was to be someone my children could point to with pride.
I didn't know it at the time, but I think a hidden reason was to
have some pride in myself and for others to think I had value as
a human being. That I wasn't a nobody. That I wasn't white
trash. I needed that desperately and I needed to hear someone to
say it to me. Let me fit in, let me belong, but at church suppers
I wanted desperate not to be noticed.

Let me work in the kitchen doing the dishes. Don't look at
me, don't see me. It would take every bit of determination I had
not to cry because I felt so inferior to everyone.

An aunt had said to me twice over the years how bad she felt
for me because my sister got all the attention. She didn't do
anything about it. I wasn't invited to her home. The only sibling
of my father to invite me to their home was my Aunt Kate. A
single mother with four children, she had lived with her father

in his house. My father had seven siblings.

It wasn't until I moved into the second foster home that I became aware of how many aunts and uncles I had. For years I was so excited about having a family that it wasn't until I was in my fifties that I realized no one had taken their brother's daughters into their home to take care of them.

One relative could have taken my sister and another could have taken me if they didn't feel they could handle two. At least, we would have been able to see each other and been with our own family members and not in foster homes. They had very little to do with us, really.

These are GOOD people so I didn't and don't understand how they explained this to themselves. I don't know how they could live in clear conscience. Maybe our parents messed up, but that wasn't my sister's or my own fault. It was an unspoken vow with my own children when they married and had children that if anything happened to one of them, someone in the family would take the children into their own home.

When three of my children were teenagers and the younger two near their teens, I had the same dream over and over. I lived with the fear that Social Services would come and take my children away from me because I was a woman alone.

Things were different back then. When my Aunt Kate and her husband separated, he got the children because she didn't have a job. He did. He also had remarried right away. She moved in with her father, took in washings and ironings, saved her money, and went to court to get her children back. I had this as an example.

In the dream, I was in hiding with my children. I would learn that Social Services was coming to take my children away from me. We would pack all we could in the car and take off. We would settle somewhere else and after awhile, when they didn't find us, I would begin to feel safe. But they always found out where we were and we would have to leave everything behind again. The dream would have me in such a state that I thought about moving to another country because NO ONE was ever going to get my children away from me.

* * *

Things had been deteriorating between Ollie and I for some time. I tried to open up a dialogue as to what was troubling me, but it didn't work. Neither of us were mature enough to handle the situation, I believe. Now, I would know what to hold on to and what to let go of in order to have accord between us.

We separated. He told his parents, who lived near by, and they came to our home. Ollie and his father were in the kitchen. My mother-in-law and I were sitting on the front porch. She turned, looked at me and told me that I was too nice to Ollie. I was surprised by the remark. She was a woman of few words. Ollie wanted out of the marriage. We divorced.

The kids and I sat on my bed and I explained Ollie's and my decision with them. They were assured they could see their father whenever they wanted to. He and I would not be having screaming matches with each other or use the children against each other. The heavy load of having to tell the children had been lifted from me, but I wasn't fully aware of the one that took its place. Total responsibility. We sat huddled on the bed and there was quiet crying by all of us.

Earlier, before I made the decision to ask for a separation, I had made an appointment to talk to the minister of our church. I spent three hours emptying myself of years of heartache and frustration. One point he made was that no one respects a doormat. Evidently, that had been my role in life or at least with

Ollie. The minister said children are better off with one parent than two if there are problems that are too deep. The children are the ones who would suffer. In a peaceful home they could continue to grow to mature adults, emotionally, and have stable lives. The line in the sand was drawn.

The children and I had use of the house until the last child was out of school. I continued to work in the satellite office of the local dry cleaning business. The pay for such work wasn't that much and with mortgage payments, utilities, house insurance, food and clothing, I was having a difficult time financially. I had to make an extremely hard decision. I could not afford to live in the house. It had to be put up for sale. We would have to find a less expensive place to live.

I also made the decision for various reasons to move to another part of the state. There was no challenge to my doing this.

A local couple we knew had moved to the Lockport, New York area and I contacted the wife about the possibilities of working in a dry cleaning office there. I requested that she send me names and addresses. She went to a phone booth and tore the yellow pages out with this information on them and mailed them to me.

There was a Montgomery Ward listed on one of the pages and I decided to consider them, too. My friend suggested applying to the Harrison Radiator plant. It was shift work. I told her I couldn't do shift work and leave the children home alone for hours at a time. She said the pay was excellent. I still said, "No."

I arranged a vacation from my job for a month away and then wrote every dry cleaning business and Montgomery Ward explaining I would be moving to the area shortly, asking for an appointment with their business. I asked customers for personal references as to my character and my work ethic. My employer gave me a good recommendation.

When I headed for Lockport, I had five interviews lined up. I went to each place with Montgomery Ward being the last on the list. They said they would hire me. I told them my children had three weeks of school left, would they possibly hold the job for me. The manager asked me if I would come then for sure and I told him that I would. I had a job but no place to live.

I had been staying that week with my friend and when I told her about the job, and that I had no place to live, she told me that me and mine could stay with her until I was able to find a place. I wanted to rent a house.

I went home, listed the house with a realtor, and went back to work at the dry cleaners. I was really praying hard the house would sell. It hadn't by the time we had to move to where my new job awaited. The realtor would keep trying to sell it.

My son stayed with his father as he had a summer job in the area, while my next to oldest daughter stayed with her cousin and the cousin's grandmother in Erie, PA. My oldest daughter, two youngest daughters, and myself made the initial move.

Before we leave Hamilton Street, I want to bring my sister's life up to date. After Ollie and I got our own apartment, I received a request from my sister asking if she could come and live with us. For reasons I will not discuss, I knew it wasn't a good idea.

I told her that Ollie and I needed to get to know each other better before we could bring someone else into our home on a permanent basis. Which was the truth. I told her she could come and spend weekends with us, because she was still going to school, over a period of time and we would go from there.

On the first weekend, something that I was afraid might happen did. I still would have let her come weekends, but her case worker said my sister was very troubled and needed special help. Help that I wasn't qualified to give her. Both my sister and I were troubled.

The next thing I heard concerning my sister was that she had gotten married and moved. I didn't know to whom or where until her soon to be ex-husband came to see me wanting her address. I didn't have it. He was in the Navy and had gotten a Dear John letter stating she was going to divorce him. He had no idea there was a problem. He needed to get in touch with her so he could get the signed divorce papers to her.

My cousin and Ollie's brother were both in the Navy at different times and told me they had seen my sister working as a waitress in a restaurant by the base in Norfolk, VA. When they spoke to her she told them they had made a mistake and that she wasn't my sister. My brother-in-law called me telling me of this exchange. He wrote my name and address on a piece of paper and gave it to her telling her this was where I was living in case she wanted to get in touch with me.

He didn't dare talk to her longer because he wasn't sure she wouldn't call the shore patrol on him and he didn't want that. He had a wife and a little girl and didn't want trouble for them, or on his record with the Navy.

Somehow, my cousin got her address and mailed it to me. I never heard from her, but I wrote her about every month for five years. I knew she got them because my return address was on every letter and none were returned to me. I kept hoping.

I was at a church meeting one evening and a phone call came for me from my home. I was told I had received a long distance phone call and the lady said she would call back at eleven. The meeting wasn't over by quarter to eleven and I sat there very afraid to get up and leave. The people would think I was rude and that my position on the board concerning the children in the church wasn't important to me. They would dismiss me.

I literally started shaking. I was sure it was my sister who had called. I finally babbled something and left. We lived about four minutes from the church. I made it in two. I was so excited. The call was from her and we talked for two and a half hours.

She was coming to my house for a week's visit. I was ecstatic and she would be here for Thanksgiving! She, a girlfriend and her little poodle arrived. There was an awkwardness on my part, but my sister seemed at ease. She conversed with her friend mostly, but I felt that was natural because it had been so long since we had communicated with each other. I told them they could use my bedroom which was on the first floor.

There were two doors to my bedroom, one across the hall from the bathroom and the other, a louvered pine door, leading into the dining room. They kept going in and out of that door, slamming it shut every time. I was concerned the slamming would loosen the slats, causing them to fallout. This fear came from the fact we could afford to buy things only once and couldn't afford to fix it if it got broke. My stomach was in knots about it and I asked her nicely to please not slam the door.

I could see what I said upset her, but she didn't say anything. The next morning, when they came out of the bedroom, they were carrying their packed suitcases. She said they were leaving and they did, but not before she told me her psychiatrist had warned her not to come because all of us up here were the cause of her emotional problems. I mentioned Thanksgiving, which was the next day, and she said they would not be staying. This was the morning of the third day at my home.

Things must have gotten straightened out because Ollie, the children and I drove to Norfolk and stayed at the home of she and her new husband, for the weekend. It went very well.

Another time, I flew to Norfolk and stayed the weekend with

she and her third husband at their home. It was a lovely home. That visit went well, also.

My second husband, two of my daughters and one of their girlfriends, and I, went to Norfolk to visit. The visit was to be for five days but we left for home on the morning of the fourth day. This visit didn't go so well.

The following Christmas, my daughters each got a Christmas card from her, but I didn't get one. In one of the girl's cards, she wrote that they could come and live with her. I had no idea where this was coming from. I wrote to my sister and told her if she couldn't send a card to everyone in the family not to send any. I received a letter from her saying that as far I was concerned she was dead. I haven't heard from her since and that was over twenty years ago.

Yes, I do feel remorse about the situation, but if not having contact with anyone up north meant she has had a happy life, known joy and contentment, then I'm happy for her. She had one child, a daughter. Her pain hurts my soul.

LOWER MOUNTAIN ROAD

Sometime during the third week of my family and I living with my friend, her boyfriend heard of a house to rent. He said it had four bedrooms, a kitchen and dining room, living room, laundry room and a full basement. The owners had quoted an asking monthly rent amount and he had gotten them down five dollars. If I was interested, he would let them know and try to get the rent even lower. I told him to tell them I accepted their amount and how soon could we move in. He told me I should try to get the rent lower. I was adamant. I accept their amount. I was appreciative of having a house to move into as my friends life style and mine were quite different. For the friendship to continue, we needed to move.

Ollie had told me to call him when I was ready to have the furniture brought up and he would see that it got done. I called. He did. His legal obligation to his children was to send a check each week. Our son remained in Penn Yan with his father. He would be starting college in the fall. Our oldest daughter was a senior in high school when we moved to our new location. That made it very rough on her. She did graduate. The next oldest daughter said it wasn't easy for her, going to a new school her junior year. She did graduate. They all graduated from high school. Three have college degrees. I'm very proud of them.

I continued to work for Montgomery Ward, but what I really wanted was to stay at home. I wanted to get the girls off to school in the morning and be there when they came home from school—so they could share their days news with me. I actually enjoyed cleaning house, doing laundry, ironing, baking, and cooking our meals.

I couldn't stay home, of course, and I gave my job 100 percent. I started as a cashier and flunky in the basement of the store. That was where the paint and plumbing supplies were located, plus tires and auto supplies. The department I was involved in was house wares. After awhile I was given a couple departments of my own on the main floor. They were yard goods, bedding, and towels. The departments were at the back of the store. The curtains, drapes, and accessories department were behind mine. The person they belonged to also had the men's wear department at the front of the store.

One day he asked me if I would mind keeping the counters looking nice because some of the ladies would take merchandise out of the plastic bags and not put it back in the bags. With him being up front, he couldn't check on it very often because it meant having to leave his main department and losing sales. I agreed to because I was to afraid to say no. I thought the other clerks would think I was wrong for not helping out a fellow worker.

His next request was to wait on the customers because I was right there and there wasn't that many curtains sold anyway ... so it wouldn't take much of my time. Then it was inventory time. Would I do his? I had my own two departments to do.

It is a very time consuming task. I finally got so upset with his arrogance and superior attitude that it overcame my timid and scared of my shadow inferiority complex, and whatever else I had going. I called the manager on our store phone system for an appointment to see him. He said for me to come right on up, which was probably a good thing, as it didn't give me time to chicken out. I knew I couldn't or this abuse would continue and maybe even get worst.

I went to the manager's office and explained what had been happening. I felt it was wrong and if I was going to do all the work, I should get the commission. Then I added, beings I was already doing all the work, that I should get the department.

I shocked myself on that part. I heard, later, that he had called the man to his office. I received notification that the department was mine. It felt good.

I continued to work hard at the store and at home. I couldn't let either place down. They got my best. I kept getting more and more tired physically, emotionally, and mentally. It never entered my mind to call in and take a sick day when I wasn't sick. I thought that was a deceitful, dishonest thing to do. I couldn't afford to lose a day's pay, anyway.

This one day, I wasn't going to let it bother me and I was going to work a little late. Just a couple hours of not having to hurry. The employees went in the back door when coming to work as the main front doors weren't open yet for the general public. I assumed my tardiness was known and the manager might be waiting for me by the back doors to catch me coming in late.

I figured to outsmart him and decided I would come in the front door and hopefully to my departments before he saw me. I went in the front door and there he was, waiting on a customer! I wasn't sure if he had seen me or not until he said, "Good afternoon, Beverly." I said, "Good afternoon." Hurriedly and meekly, I went to my departments. It was 10 a.m.

There had been rumors floating around for a month that there were going to be hours cut and layoffs. This really scared me as I had four children at home and I was the source of income. I went to the assistant manager telling him what I heard and asked if my hours were going to be cut. His answer was, "Would I do that to you, Beverly?" I felt relieved.

I had forgotten this was the man known as the manager's hatchet man and that someone had fired a pellet gun at him as he stood by the glass paneled back door, missing him only because he moved. My hours were cut. This was two days before Christmas.

I went home at lunch time and did not go back to work or go into work the next day. Nor did I call to let them know I wouldn't be coming into work. I was distraught as to what was going to happen to my children and myself. I needed every penny I made just to make ends meet.

I hated the thought of welfare because foster children are welfare. I knew if it came to that I would have to do it. I was intensely angry that I had been put in the position where I would have to put my children into the same system I had been in. I applied for unemployment and qualified for eight dollars a week. Eight dollars is better than nothing. I kept looking in the local paper for jobs that were available.

Noon of one day, I received a call from the assistant manager, who in a kind tone of voice asked me if I was going to continue working for Montgomery Ward. I was a good employee and they would hate to lose me. I agreed to because I knew I had no choice. He was so glad to hear that. Now I worked twenty hours a week. We ate a lot of soup and casseroles.

I used to say to myself if my sense of humor left I would really be in trouble. One such time it was needed was on a trip to the unemployment office, which was fifteen miles away, to do the weekly sign up.

I had a robins egg blue sport coupe Corvair which I was making two payments on—one to the bank and one to a mechanic. One day as I was driving I thought I saw smoke inside the car, then I knew I saw smoke inside my car and it kept getting worse. It was winter, so I had the windows closed, but it got so bad I had to open the window by my side and the smoke poured out. I started laughing uproariously because I knew what a sight it must have been to other people driving by and behind me.

I pulled into a car parts store parking lot and went inside to call my oldest daughter who worked in the area. She came and took me to sign up and after work took me to where I had left the car. I allowed myself to worry what it was going to cost to fix the car. I put the key in the ignition and it started. I was able to drive it home. I don't recall what the problem was but I do know it was something minor.

After about eight weeks, I received another phone call from the assistant manager telling me there was a job opening if I wanted it. It wasn't the job I had before. I would be working the in-house switchboard. I had never done anything like that in my life and insecurities came forth, but were shortly over come when he told me it was that job or no job. I figured I'd learn how to do it, keep looking at the employment section of the local daily newspaper, and when such a job was listed I'd apply for it. Part of the duties was to take customers payments on their account and at five o'clock to cash out the drawer. And you stayed with it until it balanced.

I found it to be a very boring job. There weren't that many outside calls coming in but the employees kept the switchboard jumping, wanting to be connected to a different department and to the stock room which was on the top floor of the building.

So many times—so, so, many times—the call lighting up the board would be from this one cashier station. The same clerk each time. One time a light went on and it was her station. I was so tired of repeating each and every time, "Switchboard." Then

I said, "Yeah." And the manager asked, "Would you give me the stock room, please, Beverly?" I said, "Yes sir."

No telephone operator job had been listed, but there was a job listed for help at a Montgomery Ward catalog store that would be opening in Niagara Falls. I applied. I got the job. The pay was fifteen dollars more a week. As with any new business it was slow to attract customers, so, after three weeks my boss told me that my pay would be cut fifteen dollars a week. One thing that didn't help the situation was the fact the head office sent merchandise to be placed on the floor for sale. The manager of the store had no input as to what merchandise was coming or if he even wanted it. The goods were charged to the managers account and if they didn't sell it, it was his tough luck. It didn't help his financial situation.

It really frustrated my boss and he had a temper to begin with, so I found out. A pencil sailed past my head without any warning and other sundry items. The truck bringing ordered and non-ordered items came to the back door of the stockroom and shortly after the truck door was open, I heard a verbal explosion and then something hit the opposite wall. It was an un-ordered blender. I was at the front counter waiting on a customer. Thank heavens.

I was beginning to be concerned that a flying object might hit me some day. Over the weekend, I had to go to a department store and I saw these fluorescent orange rubber balls about the size of a baseball, so I bought one. I had a plan. I wasn't sure how it would be received.

Monday morning, before the store opened for the day, I walked to where my boss was sitting at his desk and said, "Joe, I got you something. Things have been flying by my head and I'm a little concerned one of them might hit me. Here. If this hits me it won't hurt and with being so orange when you get mad again, you'll be able to find it."

I said it with a smile and in a joking way, but I still held my breath. He took it as I meant it and did aim future airborne projectiles away from me.

One morning, as I was to go to work, the weather was so bad with blizzard like conditions that I knew it would be dangerous for me to drive to work. It was time for me to leave for work and I still hadn't made up my mind whether to go or not. I was terrified to call my boss and tell him I wouldn't be coming to work that day. It wasn't because of his temper, but I was sure he would fire me.

I couldn't make the decision as to what to do. The feeling I had was totally irrational. I was incapable of making the decision. I was paralyzed by a mind that had gone into hiding. I made the call, vacillated for quite a few moments and my boss finally said, "Bev, just say you won't be in to work. I'll see you tomorrow if the weather is better." I cried with relief and shame. Why did I act this way?

My boss was used to walking around with $300 in his wallet and now he had none. He finally had enough, called headquarters, and quit that day. He walked out the door and didn't come back.

That left me in a quandary. What was I supposed to do? I was notified that the company wouldn't be able to get someone to temporarily take over for a week and would I operate the store until then, except for the paper work. Now, that didn't scare me. Go figure.

During that week, a business friend of my boss stopped in and offered to put up the five thousand dollars necessary for me to take over the franchise. I would eventually repay him. I was stunned by the offer and honored by the fact he had such confidence in me. I told him I would think about it and let him know.

I was aware it would mean eighteen-hour days at the store. I still had three children at home who needed me, especially, since they were teenagers. I told him I would be unable to accept his most gracious offer and why.

I went to work at a furniture store across the street that belonged to the cousin of my former boss. I was to do the daily bookwork and dust. I wasn't good at book work, but was great at dusting.

I did not like it there, one reason being, the cousin would come into the backroom at the catalog store and nonchalantly run his hand across my bottom. No, I didn't say anything to my boss at the time because I was sure he wouldn't believe me. I felt he wouldn't believe me over what his cousin would say. I started looking in the newspapers for another job.

I applied for a job at the Upson Company to be an addressograph operator. Hadn't a clue what that was. They explained it, offered me the job and I accepted. I gave two weeks notice and dusted for two weeks.

I worked in the first class mailroom and have never enjoyed working at a place like I did there. The personnel were pleasant. The working conditions were clean, plenty of daylight in the rooms. Later, a couple vice-presidents were more personal than personnel. I learned to operate every piece of equipment in the mailroom, plus selling stamps to employees.

One noon, a male vice-president came into the mailroom, gave me money for a certain number of stamps and said he would pick them up after lunch. He, evidently, drank his lunch. When I held out his stamps to him, he took the index finger of his right hand and poked me in my left breast and said, "The guys were all wondering if they were real."

I was stunned. All I could think to say was, "You have a nickel in change coming, but you aren't getting it." He left with his stamps.

My face felt as hot as a stove poker. I hid behind some cabinets until I could get myself under control. I was grateful there hadn't been anyone else in the room to witness my shame and I felt a lot of shame. What had I done that gave him the authority to degrade me. Now, I know the answer to that question—NOTHING.

There was another vice-president, head of advertising and publicity, that enjoyed the power of his position in the company.

Among my duties were operating the mimeograph and the off-set printing equipment. I printed materials for his projects. If the regular in-house mail person wasn't there, I took the mail to the various offices.

Whenever I would go into his office, which had two other gentlemen employees, and he was alone, he would suggest I come around to his side of the desk so we could look over the mail together. Sometimes, he would lean over his desk toward me and make kissing noises with his lips.

I always had a flip answer for his request and behavior because I didn't want trouble. I needed my job. One day, I went into his office to deliver mail and he leaned forward over his desk and made his kissy face. I leaned over and planted a kiss on his lips. I was fed up. That action threw him back in his chair and his eyes were as big as the proverbial saucer. Without a word from either of us, I turned around and left the room. He never, never ever, made any more moves on me. He was a married man. Neither did the other married man.

* * *

Sometimes, I would spend an overnight at an aunt-by-marriage's apartment, trying to help her get her life on track. My three daughters still home were teenagers by then. I explained to them how we are to help our fellow human beings in their time of need. That was how I wanted my children to grow up—to be caring, compassionate people who cared about other people, not just themselves. Plus, being women who could handle their life no matter what was thrown at them over the years.

This aunt was an emotional mess. She drank more than she should and had a great capacity to hook up with the wrong kind of man. Her life showed the effects of her decisions.

This one year she was particularly downhearted and I decided to treat her for her birthday by taking her out to eat and go to a movie. We went to a nice restaurant and then to the movie *Funny Girl.* The cost of the tickets were double what they usually were. I saw casseroles for the girls and I for the next week.

After the movie, I drove her to her apartment. There was a corner bar across the street and she wanted to go for a nightcap. I said, "No." But I was sure she would go there as soon as I turned the corner. I figured she would be better off with me with her. I told her it would be for a short time.

She sat at a stool at the bar and ordered a green liquid on the rocks. To me, sitting at a bar was unlady like. I saw table and chairs and was going to suggest sitting there. I ordered a sweet daiquiri. The bartender said, "This ain't uptown lady." I said, "I'll have what she's having."

I did suggest table and chairs, but it was turned down. I saw a long, narrow table and asked what it was. It was some kind of a game and she showed me how to play it. I'm a sipper of liquids, so we were there longer than I wanted to be. If I pay for something, I'm finishing it.

We walked to my car. I watched her go into the building, continued to sit there for awhile until I was quite certain she was in for the night. She couldn't see me from her apartment.

81

One year right after Thanksgiving, I received a call from her saying things were really bad. She needed to get out of the area. I cared what happened to her, so I offered our home to stay in as she could find a job locally and get her own place, and live happily ever after.

A man from work offered to get a truck and take me to load her stuff and bring it to our home. The truck he got was a company truck without permission and I had visions of being in jail. There was only one seat in the truck, the one the driver sat on. I sat on a pile of tires. When we got back to our place and unloaded, it was five in the morning and the both of us had to go to work in a few hours. I had to go to her friends apartment on Sunday to get her, personally.

She answered an employment ad about a job as a nanny. The home was in a nearby village where moneyed people lived. There were two children, the hours were from seven to five, and use of the swimming pool, one of the cars, and vacations with them, along with a   room of her own and seventy-five dollars a week wages, was offered. It was ideal.

She said she had to think about it, deciding she didn't want to be tied down that much. When she told me that I stared at her with my mouth wide open, thinking what is wrong with this woman. How can she live off a single woman with three children to support. After the initial shock wore off, I counseled her saying she could take this job and keep looking for one that she might like, at least making money to buy a car and whatever she wanted. She wouldn't do it.

The day before Christmas, I received a call at work from her. She was going back to where she used to live. This fella called her telling her how much he missed her and wanted her with him. He wanted her to move in with him. She was going back. I felt my friendship had been betrayed.

I said through clenched teeth, "You will spend Christmas with us, of course." To which she said, "No, I'm leaving today." I asked her how she was going to get there? I wasn't taking her. He was coming to pick her up. I told her I would not move her stuff back. She said that he would and I told her to make it soon. Five weeks had gone by and I still had her stuff, which included furniture. I called her and said to come and get her things or the Salvation Army would. They came. I could see she had absolutely no guilt over how she had acted. I couldn't figure that out.

About a week after she was gone from the house, my children told me how she would ask them if they smoked marijuana. They told her no, but she wouldn't believe them as all teenagers did. One of my daughters said she did (the clown of the family) and had some at the house. Would she like her to make one for her. Of course, the answer was in the affirmative.

The girls went into the kitchen, looking through my spices, got a sheet of toilet tissue and made a cigarette. They took it to her and she lit it up. The girls were amazed it burned. She sat there puffing away and once she mentioned it tasted like whatever spice it was they had used to make it. They lost all respect for her. If she had been living there when the girls told me, I'm not sure what I would have done. It would have been dramatic for such actions involving my children. I was furious. I was shaking with anger. She was out of our lives forever.

* * *

Life went on. It bothered me that the girls were alone at home from when they got home from school until I got home from work. The girls had chores to do, but kids are kids and I was well aware of that. A lot of Fridays, I would come home to spend supper with them as I worked late that day. I had to drive home and back to work, so I only had about twenty minutes with them.

I wallpapered the walls to make our home attractive, took care of a big yard, had a garden each year to can and freeze from, made jam, had to find someone to plow the garden, and had to find someone to do to everything I couldn't and that required a lot of time and energy. There were school meetings to go to ... some good, some not so good. I took the not so goods as my fault for not being home more. I was failing in my place as their mother.

I wanted to give the girls a balanced life which meant having a party now and then. We had one in the barn which was on the grounds where we lived. It was a fairly new barn and had been used only to store bee hives over the winter months. There was plenty of food, music and dancing. Everyone had a good time.

I had a Christmas party for some adults from work at the house. I kept a cupboard fairly stocked with liquor because I thought that was what you were supposed to do from listening to people and reading magazines.

At one time, when I was talking to a woman I worked with I realized that I was acting. Acting, because I did not know how to socially interact. I used words I thought I should say. I morphed into another persona because I am barren of real emotions for this situation. A sense of disassociation. There is something missing from my growing up experiences and it still haunts me.

* * *

There were four happenings while we lived at Lower Mountain Road that have no explanation as far as I'm concerned. Two were of terror, two were of overwhelming peace. One night, I was awaken by a feeling of an evil presence in the room. I was literally frozen with terror. I could not speak or move. I was sure something terrible was going to happen to me. My Sundays at the Baptist Church, as a child, brought a thought to mind. If I could utter the name Jesus Christ whatever it was couldn't stand up against that and would go away. I tried and tried to get the Lord's name out but no sound came out of my mouth. I kept trying and first it was a whisper, then louder and louder, never a shout, but enough so I could feel the evil slowly leave the room.

This happened one more time and I did as before. The next time, I was awaken by the most overwhelming sense of peace I had ever known. I took it to be my earthly father guaranteeing me that he was watching over me, keeping me safe. I now believe it was my other, holy, father.

The last time, I was standing in the backyard, the sun came out brilliantly, and peace settled on me like a cloak. I have no understanding what the reason was behind these events.

I received a telephone call one day from Ollie's brother telling me Ollie had died suddenly of a heart attack. I screamed and then cried. Although, we were divorced that doesn't mean you want to see your former spouse dead. He was only 43.

I cried for our children. I wanted to pass to someone else the responsibility of telling them their father had died. I didn't know if I could handle the pain and anguish that would come from their feelings of devastation. There was no one else to tell them. I have no recollection as to what I said or when I said it. I believe it was too painful to retain in my memory.

Every month, I received a monthly check from the government for dependent children and it made the difference from my going on welfare or not because no matter how much I disliked the thought of welfare, losing my children wasn't an option. My son's amount went to him to help with his college expenses.

I did something that many questioned my sanity over. I bought an inexpensive riding horse. I believed it was a living creature that the children could use to give love and attention to, and in some way help keep a positive outlook on life. I bought a western saddle and we all took our turn riding our horse. We named her Lady.

Of course, I could have just let our kitten and cat population grow. I counted the feline population one day and there were fourteen. The girls, off and on, would say they found abandoned kittens in our yard, along the road, and in other places where it was dangerous to leave them.

After I counted the number of cats, I told them I didn't care where they found them, no more cats! It wasn't until everyone was grown up and living on their own that I found out these furry pets were being rescued from the local SPCA. The girls knew that after animals have been there for a certain period of time, if no one takes them, the animals are put to death. They wanted to save as many as they could.

About 300 feet from the house was a culvert that went under the highway. The girls and the neighbor kids played in the creek that flowed through it, a lot. I was in the house and a daughter came running in asking me to come outside and see what they had.

They had taken the large plastic garbage can that had a metal bail handle, which was being held in the air by a small tree branch, that was held by another daughter of mine. I thought I would see frogs, tadpoles, minnows, something along that line. I was totally unprepared for what I did see. A snake. I hate snakes and this one made my center go dead calm.

It looked like a rattlesnake. I heard a whirring sound. It's tail was moving. The thought surged through my mind if that thing got out of there the possibility of a child or more than one getting bitten was a certainty. I calmly told my daughter to hand the stick to me and to quickly get the can of gasoline that we kept for the lawn mower.

I told another daughter to go in the house and get the box of farmer matches we had for burning the trash. I slowly walked the garbage can toward a concrete pad by the outdoor pump, shaking the can as I went because the snake was trying to slither up the sides.

I instructed my daughter to take the cap off the gas can and hold it near me. I instructed my other daughter to take a match out of the box and to hold the box and match near me. I figured I didn't have much time to act once I set the garbage can down on the concrete pad. I set it down and grabbed the gas can, pouring the liquid into the plastic can, believing it would disorient the snake to give me time to light the match and toss it in the can.

I yelled, "Get back." I threw in the lighted match. There was a ball of fire. No more garbage can, no more snake. Then, I went into hysteria. When the girls learned the truth of the situation, so did they. I don't know if there are any other snakes that have rattles, but at that point I didn't care. I found out from neighbors that a number of years earlier there had been such snakes in the area. The consensus was that somehow they got brought in when major work was being done on the highway. My heart still gets gripped by fear when I think about it, which I try very hard not to do.

For three years after we moved to Lower Mountain Road, my life consisted of going to work and being home. One day, I found myself giggling silly with the girls and thinking exactly like them. I had cut off the outside world and realized, for all our sakes, I had better join the adult world.

There was a woman who worked where I did and we got to be

friendly. She was in the same situation as I was in regards to the fact she was raising five children by herself. Her husband had moved out and took care of all expenses for the family.

She liked to go out on the weekend. Her mother would come and stay overnight. We would go out on a Friday or Saturday night. We went dancing and, of course, these places served alcoholic drinks. I had never done anything like this and found I liked dancing very much. This lasted for about a year and I got to where I didn't care for the other stuff that went with the dancing. I talked to a gentleman that I knew about how I felt like a piece of meat when I went to these places, like I was being sized up as to—will she or won't she.

He told me I had the scene right. We always went to a nice place, but as far as I'm concerned the only difference between a nice place and a dive are the words used. I left that scene, but not soon enough. I had met my second husband, to be.

My thinking went like this. I had read how a male figure in a home is very important in little girls lives for their being able to have good relations with the male gender. He was ten years younger than me, but I knew that wouldn't be a problem. Evidently, someone in his family didn't feel the same way because I received a letter that had a clipped out cartoon in it and the caption under the picture stated—he must like antiques because he married one. He worked steady. He drank more than I knew he did.

A brother and sister-in-law of his had split up and their house was available to buy. He wanted to buy it. I didn't think .it was a good idea to live by parents, but I was over ruled. We paid his parents $3,000 for the taxes they had paid on the house to keep it off the delinquent tax rolls. He didn't get a receipt from his parents and I told him I thought we should.

It was common sense. He got angry and said you don't get receipts from relatives. A few years later that decision came back to haunt me. We went to the family lawyer and the house was ours. We moved my furniture into our home.

THE AKRON ROAD YEARS

The house hadn't been totally finished. The upstairs half-bath was just studs, the entrance to the basement was a hole in the floor covered with loose boards at one end of the kitchen, the fireplace never worked, the floors had tile squares, the basement was full of water and chunks of ice, the siding was coming off in spots, and the lawn was nothings but clumps of grass.

A broken down home made and an above ground swimming pool was in the back yard. Enough work had been done to make it livable. When spring came, I mowed the lawn twice a week. After about five weeks it began to look like a decent lawn.

We had carpeting put on the living room floor. That helped to improve the look of things somewhat. My husband pumped the water out of the basement and I helped him make concrete steps to go to the basement, which had to start from the inside wall of the attached garage. The hole in the kitchen floor was made part of the rest of the floor.

He started going out at night, at first, and then when he had days off he came home drunk. It took me awhile before the thought came to me that this marriage of ours wasn't what he wanted. I came to the conclusion the age difference between us did matter. We weren't on the same track as to what our future plans were. I filed separation papers. He was delighted when he was handed those papers. He later remarried and they had children.

The process of obtaining a lawyer began. My husbands family

all used the same lawyer for their legal affairs, so that lawyer had a big stake in the outcome. He was in practice in a small city where every lawyer knew each other.

My youngest child still had a couple years of high school left, so we were able to remain in the house, with the stipulation that as soon as she graduated I had to buy my husband's share of the house. If I couldn't come up with the money or a mortgage, the house would be sold. This was his lawyer's words. I talked to people I knew and they told me that is how it usually worked.

About a year before my daughter was to graduate, I went to a local lawyer to find out what my chances were for getting a mortgage on the house. He told me my chances were pretty much nil. I asked why? He told me because I was single, the bank's line of reasoning would be—I would get pregnant and not able to work, therefore, I wouldn't be able to make my payments, or that I would marry someone who wouldn't do his part in our relationship, and I wouldn't be able to make the payments.

I told him that I couldn't accept that, expecting to lose the retainer fee I had paid him. I had no idea where I would come up with money for another retainer fee. He gave the retainer fee to me. I hired another lawyer. He was gung-ho when I first met him. He asked who my husband's lawyer was? I told him. Four weeks went by and I hadn't heard from him. I spent those weeks vacillating, should I call him or not because he might get very angry at me and that he would call me when he was ready to. I did call him. My whole body was shaking with anxiety.

He took my call telling me there wasn't much he could do for me. I approached the subject of having to pay him a retainer fee and he told me no as he hadn't done any work on my case.

I thought about what the first lawyer had told me and began to look for a second job. I was determined to fight what I considered an unfair assessment of women.

I was hired to work in the kitchen of a local restaurant. My thought was, now I could afford to make the payments and the bank's loan officer would see what a hard worker I was and how resourceful and dependable I was.

In the tenth month of working two full time jobs I went to a savings and loan bank to talk to the man in charge of issuing mortgages. I told him what I had been told by the lawyer about my chances of obtaining a mortgage and he nodded his head and said that was pretty accurate. Then I told him that first off I couldn't get pregnant, and second, with my schedule, who the hell had time for a man? He chuckled. I took that as a somewhat good sign. He said he had to talk with board members of the bank and would get back to me.

I kept going home on my lunch hour to check my mail. This one day there was a letter from the bank. I didn't want to be alone when I opened it, so I took it back to work. I had confided in another employee about what had been going on, took her aside, and opened the letter. I read it and squeezed my lips and eyes together to keep from crying out loud, then I handed the letter to her.

I had been approved for the mortgage. I had never been so happy in my life, nor had such a sense of thankfulness. Not only did I not have to find another place for my daughter and I to live, but I had a HOME where my married children and their children could come and visit me. Again, to be on a level playing field with their grown-up friends.

I didn't want them to be ashamed of me. I wanted them to be proud of me. There was a big yard where a lot of playing could go on. Thanksgiving and Christmas dinners could be shared.

An appointment was set up for my soon-to-be husband to go to the bank and sign papers. Shortly before the meeting, I received a letter from the family lawyer stating that my former father-in-law wanted $3,000 for taxes he had paid on the house and property. If I couldn't come up with the money the house would have to be sold. I wrote to the lawyer informing him that the man had already been paid for the taxes. Did I have a signed receipt? Of course, I didn't.

I have had some bouts of depression through the years, but this was the worst. To have come so close. I called an older couple I knew and talked to the wife and cried out my story. They were people of great faith and I needed to communicate with someone like that because I was so angry. We talked and she said she would call me back. She did, they would loan me the money. I paid them ninety dollars a month for three years, plus the regular mortgage payment. It was difficult to do, but I got to keep my home and my ex-husband got his money. I lived there for 20 years.

After another month, I quit my job at the restaurant. Working two jobs—caring for my child, plus taking care of the house and all that goes with it—was proving too much for me, physically. I continued to work at the tax map job.

It was an interesting job. Every inch of land in New York State had to be accounted for—who owned it. It was discovered some of it was owned, but not listed on the tax rolls, which was part of the reason to do this. The president of the company would negotiate with various counties for the contract to plot their land. The company had their own plane and camera operator. They would fly over the entire county taking photographs, coming back, developing the film into twelve-inch squares.

One group of employees would take the photos and draw on strips of mylar where tree lines, creeks, hedgerows, roads and other pertinent objects were. These pieces of mylar were in sections and given to other employees whose job it was to draw in each parcel of property as to who owned it using the photographs and the deeds that had been photocopied at the county. It was extremely difficult to do because so many deeds were from many years ago with descriptions such as: go so many chains, links from the center of a highway to a tree with three hacks on it, then to a pile of rocks, and then to the center of the highway. That's where using the photographs helped. We had magnifying glasses, which we bought ourselves. When our part of the project was finished, the mylars were taken on to the next phase, being transferred to paper which eventually were taken to the county when everything was completed.

The lady who was manager quit and I was given that position. I was put on salary and spent many hours making our part of the operation more efficient. I was able to convince the president of the company to give the employees a morning 10-minute coffee break. We did not have a break throughout the day. He would not allow an afternoon break. We could eat our lunch at our table and keep working if we wanted to.

I figured as long as business was the way my life was going to play out, I should get a degree to put on my resume, if needed, in the future. I discussed this with the president of the company and he said I would be reimbursed for each semester I finished with passing grades. We had a debate sometimes if certain jobs pertained to my job. I had to take two social sciences (first aid and fencing) which I knew was out of bounds for reimbursement. I went part time and it took me four years to graduate. I was 51.

My soon-to-be third husband's wife worked in the same room as me. She was a very argumentative woman. We would meet her husband now and then thinking there couldn't be a nicer guy. One day, she was called down to the first floor and she came back with her brown bag lunch she had forgotten to bring to work.

Her husband had brought it in to her. She was red in the face, she was so mad. All the wives said they would give anything if their husband would do something like that. They told her this and she got even more upset.

On the weekends, I would work on remodeling the house. It was a split level house and over the attached garage was one large room, going from the front of the house to the back of the house, and three teeny bedrooms. They consisted of rough lumber thrown together to make bunk beds, with teeny closets attached to the head of the bunk beds. With a dresser in the room there was no more space.

I opened the windows and proceeded to knock the bunk beds apart, throwing the wood out the windows. I took out one dividing wall and looked at the other one. It needed to come out but I wasn't sure if it would be all right to take it out. Would the roof cave in? It seemed to me the main beam went from front to back so I took it out. The roof stayed in place. Now, I did have a dilemma. How do you put up a new wall?

I talked about it at work and the wife of my future husband said he was real handy with mechanics and carpentry. She told me to ask him. I asked, why didn't she ask him? Her answer was that he was more willing to do things if someone asked rather then her. That seemed odd, to me. I asked him and he finally said he would. He did and I watched him and afterwards thought, I could have done that. So, I made two double wide closets and hung the folding doors. I put drywall on the new wall and all that goes with that job. I had a sense of accomplishment.

At the same time, I worked on landscaping the yard. I had no one to help me and no rototiller to use, so I hand-spaded every flower bed of which there were many. After I did the spading, I would get down on the ground and use a small hand tool to knock off the sod of the clumps of grass, then I had to get rid of the grass.

I put in places in the yard that were low. I would plant either plant roots or seeds. I absolutely love flowers, particularly, the old-fashioned ones like holly-hocks, bleeding heart, forsythia, red quince, and zinnias.

I planted peach trees, a sour cherry tree, pear trees, elderberry bushes, blueberry bushes, red raspberry bushes, and strawberries. Also, asparagus and rhubarb. I did hire someone to rototill a small space for a vegetable garden. This was done so we could have fresh fruit without having to pay the high prices in the stores or roadside stands. I also froze and canned things for the winter when heat and electric costs were high.

I dug the full length of the driveway and planted myrtle and a flowering almond bush. My home and property were becoming what I wanted, for me. I was trying to make the ideal home I never had but always wanted. There was never enough money, but I had a sense of joy and accomplishment.

I had help building a small barn and by doing that I learned how to use power tools. It came in handy over the years. One day we were working on putting the siding on the barn and after my husband left for the afternoon shift, I kept working. I wanted to get this side finished. Your eyes seem to adjust as dusk comes and I could still see what I was doing, only I was more tired than I thought.

I was standing on a scaffold when I felt a tug on my pant leg. I looked down and saw a 12-inch slit in the leg of my pants. Luckily, I hadn't been cut. The circular saw was still running. I hadn't let go of the power button. I let go, pulled the plug, got off the scaffolding and went into the house. Such an incidence never happened again.

The barn had been built for the horse I had purchased and our Billy goat. I have to tell you about the goat. My birthday is in

July and this one year, on the day of my birthday, the girls asked if they could borrow the car. I thought they wanted to get me a birthday gift, so I said yes. They came back after awhile and got out of the car with nothing in their hands.

I wondered just what was going on. They told me to come to the trunk of the car, my present was in there. Imagine my surprise when they opened the trunk and saw a baby goat. "We got you a baby goat," they said, "for your birthday."

I was in shock because a goat had never, ever entered my mind. I wondered just whose gift this goat was. Someone named him Baa Haa. He did provide us with many hours of entertainment, like running full tilt at the back of the house, running up the side of the house, do a flip and land on his feet, and then do it again. He had horns and would butt us sometimes, never enough to hurt, just enough to get our attention.

Lady and Baa Haa were in the barn all day as the kids were in school and I worked full time. When the weather got warm enough they were staked in the field across the road to eat, get sunshine and fresh air. We would always bring them back to the barn at night. There was a large, round metal tub that was kept full of water. They would drink their fill every morning and evening.

My neighbors, husband and wife, were fanatic animal lovers. They loved my dog and lured her away by feeding her prime food, like steak. I kept calling her home and she kept going back. She, finally, wouldn't come home.

I got another dog and they started to do the same thing. I called them on it and they left our dog alone. I did get a call one day from the wife telling me her husband was very upset because we weren't out every morning watering the animals.

I explained when we watered the animals and fed them. She

said she would tell her husband. I got a call from her, at my place of work, telling me her husband said he was going to turn me into the authorities because I don't take care of my animals.

I was furious! One reason was because she called me at work. I went home at lunch time and called the SPCA—explaining what had transpired with my neighbors—and asked them to please come to my home at any time of the day and check out my animals, and if they found anything to let me know and I would correct it. They sounded astounded but said they would.

I then called my neighbor informing her of what I had just done. She said that hadn't been necessary, but she would tell her husband when he got back. I asked where he was and she said up in Canada HUNTING ELK. Otherwise, killing an animal.

In a few days I got a letter from the SPCA letting me .know all my animals were fine. They had even checked the dog and cats. I made a copy of the letter and sent it to my neighbors. They found no fault anymore.

I noticed Baa Haa had been acting listless. I was worried that he might be sick, got a vet to come to the house, and he said he was lonesome, that animals get lonely, too. The kids were at an age where playing with a goat wasn't that much fun anymore. I heard about someone who had a female goat and wanted another one to keep her company. I called and they would take Baa Haa. I told them he couldn't sire any baby goats and that was no problem to them. I felt better when they called me and told me Baa Haa was going nuts! He was having a grand time, showing off like crazy.

Then, of course, that meant I had a horse that was probably going to feel lonely. I looked in the local penny saver to find an inexpensive horse to keep her company. There were no inexpensive horses, but there was a female colt that was going cheap. I went to their place to look it over—don't know why as I didn't know a lot of particulars about horses. I'm the one whose question was, "What's her name?" when we went to look at Lady. The man told me, "Anything you want to call her, lady."

The young friend of my daughter had a horse and she asked things about fetlocks and so on. I bought the colt and they delivered her to my home.

She wasn't trained at all and I took that on as my cause. I bought a book on the subject and read it. I bought a buggy whip to tap her on the front of her legs as they said to, at certain commands. I put a halter on her and took her out to the side yard and began. I don't recall all the instructions but I was to say stop, then tap on the front of her front legs. The very first time it worked, as a matter of fact, it worked every time

I literally asked her if she had read the book. I didn't go any further with it because only one daughter was still home and had no interest in either horse. Having a horse is expensive. You have to buy hay, straw, grain, have a vet check them regularly, and a blacksmith to check their hooves. I just couldn't afford it, especially, just to stand in a barn.

A young couple brought their twelve-year-old daughter to look at the colt and she fell in love with her. I knew she would have a good home. Lady was a different situation. She was older and I had concerns as to who would want her. Someone from a riding stable contacted me, saying they would like to add her to their stable of horses. I had bought a western saddle and they would buy that, too.

A deal was made. The night they came for her I expressed a worry that had crept into my mind. I asked them if they were really going to take her to a glue plant because if they were the deal was off. They assured me they weren't and I received confirmation later from someone I knew that she was indeed at the riding stables. I cried for a number of days after she left. I rode her many times, myself, and she was a lady, for sure—reddish color, golden mane and when she ran, her tail arched beautifully.

* * *

My life wasn't all work. There was this time when a young grandson had gotten a SMALL bright yellow tent for his birthday and I offered to sleep in it with him, on a Saturday night, in my back yard. The plan was to get a fire going on the grill the next morning and we would cook breakfast.

We put the sleeping bags in the tent and crawled inside at dusk. We talked for a little while and he blissfully went to sleep. Not I.

It seemed the tent roof was inches above my face and I would have a suffocating feeling, and I would reach up, putting my hand on the roof, so I could get a true image as to how far away it was—close my eyes, then take my hand away.

Our calico cat, Cecelia, came in and laid on my grandson, purring up a storm. Another thing not conducive to helping me get to sleep. I shooed her away and went to sleep. What woke me up was Cecelia laying on my chest, purring up a storm. I thought, what the heck, and left her there. Good news accompanied my waking up; it was raining. We cooked breakfast on the kitchen stove. I never was good at starting fires in the grill.

One afternoon, while we still had the horses, you could see in the sky that a bad rainstorm was headed our way. A couple daughters ran across the road to get the horses, to take them to the barn. Lady was no problem. My other daughter got the colt and she definitely had a problem. My daughter was only 5- foot and the colt knew it was going to the barn.

My daughter was holding on the halter and was literally

digging the heels of her shoes in the ground trying to slow the colt down. As she went by us we heard her use words we didn't even know she knew. This was my shy daughter. We were in hysterics by the time she came into the house and between burst of laughter we told her what we saw and heard.

We expected her to join in, but it didn't happen. She was mad and proceeded to let us know just how mad. It was some time before she saw the humor in it.

Except for having to let go of the horses, my life had never been so happy. If only I had been secure enough in my own mind to see it.

The wife of my soon-to-be husband had left him and moved in with another man. All of us at work thought she was a fool to leave him.

"Hello, Bev, this is xxxxxx. Would you go out with me.

"You're married."

"Separated."

"But you're still married."

"If I call when I'm not, will you go out with me?"

"Call me then."

"Okay."

THE THIRD HUSBAND

We had dates. The first one was at a nice restaurant.

Our wedding day was a month away when I got a phone call at work. I figured it had to do with a pick up truck as he had been looking at them. They wouldn't approve his application because he didn't have any collateral. Would I sign the application, putting my house up as collateral? After all, we were going to be married in a month. I admit to a moments hesitation with my mind whirling with questions. He had always been a decent guy, he worked a steady full time job, he didn't drink, and the truck would be a benefit to us.

I agreed. I went with him to pick up the truck. It was a Ford 150 with two gas tanks, black and red and in excellent condition.

We were married by a Justice of Peace with my oldest daughter and her husband as witnesses. We had a reception at a local restaurant, that my children had reserved, for both of our families.

We started off our married life with my refinancing the mortgage on the house. We did the work ourselves. We bought a new sink for the two bathrooms and two new toilets. New tile was put on the floor of the upstairs half bath, with wallboard put on the studs, and a door was hung.

A new wall protector was installed around the downstairs bath tub. The wall between the kitchen and bedroom was taken out, leaving only a center section. That room became a dining room. There were no outside steps leading from the kitchen sliding glass door to the ground, so some rough lumber was nailed together until a later date.

The next major project was to take off the pressed wood siding and replace it with four-by-eight sheets of texture 1-11. I helped measure and cut the wood. I held the four by eight sheets in place while my husband did the nailing. I stained it a chestnut brown.

I have a fear of heights and when it came to the two-story part of the house, I was a little apprehensive. I put the extension ladder up against the house, making sure the hooks were over the rungs and it was tied off. Up I went, paint can and brush in my hand. I had heard that you shouldn't look down in such a situation. I did once and had to close my eyes and lean in against the ladder until the vision went out of my mind. I didn't do that again. Yes, indeed, all this sure did increase the value of the house.

The next year it was the septic system. The tank was a handmade, concrete job and the leech lines were clay tiles. Every so often there would be a horrible smelling black spot in the side yard. The very minimum that needed doing was to install new leech lines. There were three.

A daughter dug the new ditches, adding another 25 feet to each line. The clay tiles, many of them broken, were removed and new white 10- foot plastic pipe was laid in the ditch on top of #2 stone and that was as far as the project got because cold weather was coming.

When warm weather came the next year the decision was made, not by me, to put new roofing shingles on. I had refinanced the house, again.

I shingled half the roof. I even carried one new bundle of shingles up the extension ladder. I am five-foot-two. That ranked as one of the dumbest things I ever did. It weighed about what I did. I refused to get anymore. You could look at the house and see dollar signs now.

The old broken down and handmade concrete swimming pool had been hauled away leaving a 22-foot diameter concrete pad. Instead of busting it up and having to haul it away, I suggested we use it for outdoor furniture and a grill. Then, my husband said a roof should be built over it and as we had some money left from the last refinancing, so we decided to do it. Eight two-by-fours were placed around the outside edge of the pad. They weren't placed in cement.

Help came to build the roof in my son, my son-in-law, and a friend. The helpers said a center brace was needed to give the roof stability. My husband said it didn't. Majority reigned, thank heavens. He was mad about it, but didn't show it until later and did so quite verbally, to me. The leech lines still hadn't been filled in.

I started hearing about having our own business for when my husband retired. A sharpening service. He didn't want to live hand-to-mouth when he retired. I thought that way looking to our future and agreed in general. We really needed to think about it in its entirety with competition and legal issues involved, and about where to locate the business, along with sole proprietorship, corporation, suppliers and so on. None of that happened.

His brother, who lived about a two-hour drive away, had just gotten into this line of work. We made the trip to where he and his family lived. My husband and I went to the second floor of the barn, on their property, where he had the sharpening equipment. It looked complicated to me, but I thought it was a male thing and my husband would learn how to do it.

They decided we would make a trip up once a week, so my husband could learn how to operate the equipment. We would go up after he got done with work, which made it very late when we got home. My daughter would be home alone all that time and I didn't like that, but I was expected to learn some of the stuff. My husband had started to get some items to sharpen from the guys he worked with, so we would take that work with us.

I talked to my husband about setting up our own customer base, so we would be ready to go when we got our own equipment. We got a few more customers and would go to my brother-in-laws, with him doing most of the sharpening. Our customers had to wait a week to get their sharpened work. They weren't too happy about that time frame.

I said it was time we started looking into purchasing our own equipment, but he saw no reason to do so. We were getting a few more customers. I was getting nervous. I felt we couldn't get a stable customer base by keeping on doing things as we were now.

The brother-in-law got in touch with us saying they were moving south because of his regular job. We had customers and now we didn't have equipment. I really panicked. I thought it should be awhile before he would be able to restart his business where they were moving too, so maybe the equipment could be brought to our home, allowing us to keep sharpening.

This should give us enough time to start getting our own equipment. I mentioned this idea to my husband and he said it sounded like a good idea. I had to keep after him to mention it to his brother. He finally did. The answer was no, then it changed to yes. We were to take over his payments for three months. He figured he would be ready for it by then. Ninety-three dollars a month.

The equipment went into the basement of the house. It was a wet basement with small windows at ground level. The end of three months was coming up and nothing had been done about getting our own equipment. All the work and money that had gone into this project, plus a growing customer base, for nothing.

I always kept my word.. When I started something, I finished it. My character would be in question, meaning I was of no importance once again. I couldn't take going back to square one again. I would be considered welfare riff raff, white trash, a failure. It didn't bother my husband.

It was an oh well kind of attitude with him. I struggled with trying to come up with a solution to the problem. Then, we received a telephone call from the brother-in-law. He decided not to start up a sharpening service and asked if we wanted to buy the equipment. Praise the Lord, fits in here. I told my husband, "Yes, we do." The three months we had paid on it was to come off his asking price. He would have had to pay storage if we hadn't taken it before.

That was met with resistance by both my husband and his brother. I persevered. It was finally agreed to and I began to take full breaths. I realized I had a serious problem at home. If the business was to succeed it would be up to me.

I learned to use every piece of equipment we had. It was starkly brought to focus one evening. My husband was working the night shift and there were twelve chain saw blades to have ready for the next morning. They hadn't been started on by the time he left for work. He called me at 11 p.m., asking me what were we going to do about the chain saw blades? I told him I had been working on them and had six to go. He said he knew I would be doing them. That had been his plan. They were done before I went to bed for the night.

As a matter of fact, not only did I do the household chores and sharpening, I did every aspect of the business. Bookkeeping, the advertising, getting drop points located at places of business (10), making out the billing slips, making phone calls, purchasing supplies, waiting on customers, sweeping the floor, and cleaning the equipment. I hand made Christmas cards for our customers. This is not to impress anyone, this is the facts.

The business grew slowly. I knew for it to make a decent living for us something more was needed. There was a need for someone in the community to repair small hand tools and lawn mowers. We advertised these services and business started coming in.

My husband was in agreement about doing this but when he got into it, decided he didn't like it and it petered out, leaving a bad mark on our business reputation. I am not mechanically inclined, basically, so I was no help there.

I did take electric hedge shears apart putting the blades in a hot water and lye bath to clean off the sap from the bushes, then I used a handled brush on them to get off anything left. The circular saw blades were done the same way and then hung on a rod to dry before they were sharpened. Anything that could be went through that process. I took handsaws apart and used a hand sander to get off residue and rust. I got many remarks from customers that they looked almost new. Every item was sharpened and wrapped in paper, so the fine edges didn't get nicked off in order to keep the customer from being cut.

It was decided that the piece of equipment that could do carbide tipped saw blades, drill bits and router bits would be an asset to our business. The name of our business was, The Sharpening Shop. That said it all. Two signs, with a magnetic back, were made and placed on the two front doors of our car.

There was a two-day training session at the company where we bought our equipment, Foley. It was in the Twin Cities. We scheduled a date, paid the fee and went. I listened to the description given by the instructor and watched while my husband practiced on the equipment. I thought when we had this equipment in our own shop he would become more efficient. He didn't. Many blades came back because the new tips had come off. The torch you had to use scared me immensely, so I knew I couldn't help. He would redo them. I knew it was hurting business. I didn't know what to do about it. We paid about $4,000 for this piece of equipment. What we didn't need was negative feed back.

The shop was set up in the basement of the house. My husband worked three shifts, so this meant there were many hours I was in the basement alone. I mentioned how anxious that made me feel as 99 percent of the customers were men. I was told I was being paranoid.

One day, one of the steady customers came for his sharpened work. He grabbed me and tried to kiss me. I was able to get away from him and grabbed a near by circular saw blade. We were alone. He said that he was sorry, it was just that I was such a nice person.

The feelings of white trash kept me from making the normal response of threatening to call the police. They wouldn't believe me. What I did say was, "And I intend to stay that way."

Why did men think they could do this to me and that it was all right. It had to be something I was doing. Did I look like a slut? I was most fortunate he was not a violent man. He apologized for his actions and left. His wife came after that. We converted the attached two-car garage into the new shop.

The customers liked the new arrangement. I was ecstatic about it. The table where we handled the customers transactions was placed in a way that would keep space between me and the customers.

I started to notice, my husband did less and less of the sharpening. He hadn't thought about the whole scheme of things as far as owning your own business was concerned. He had a different vision than I did. Now, it comes out his idea was a lackadaisical, work when the mood strikes, kind of business. It was like how he was always saying we would build a Florida room onto the dining room.

He kept saying it and after a year of that I asked him when this was going to happen? He was always saying this to his family and friends, so I wanted to know. He told me it was all just talk, how you just say things to make conversation. He said to me once, in a surprised tone of voice that I was the same person walking on the street as I was at home. I told him I thought everyone was. He said, they weren't. That surprised me.

We bought, on time, a number of other pieces of equipment that would make the business more competitive, about $5,000 worth. I truly believed this was going to be our retirement income.

We went to my families homes or they came to ours for the holidays. We went to his family for casual visits. They would all be talking among themselves and I sat there feeling I wasn't important enough to be included in the conversation. I felt panic at my silence. I felt hot with embarrassment and near tears and thought now that's all I need to do to totally humiliate myself.

While sitting at our kitchen table, my mother-in-law said how lovely the house looked now that my husband had put a lot of money into it. I told her the money came from my financing my house. She seemed surprised and had been sure he was putting up the money. I didn't recognize, at the time, the significance of those words.

* * *

On an evening, we went to visit a young cousin of his and his wife. She was what used to be called a ditzy blonde. She was pretty and a nice person. She asked my husband how come he didn't come to see her anymore. He used to come a lot. He said he didn't and she kept saying, he did. It was the same when we were going to his brother's home.

Every time we visited, she prepared a super meal. His brother asked her at one meal, how come they only ate like this when my husband came to their home? She looked flustered. We had a Christmas party at our house in which his friends and a young couple, who were relatives of his, came. He spent the evening sitting on the fireplace hearth with his cousin's wife. I sat by myself. I didn't want to believe what I was beginning to think. I planned on being married the rest of my life.

He told, one time, that I loved with my mind. That struck home with me because I had begun to question my capacity to love. I didn't hug my children, I talked. I reasoned, I did things with them. Was I really a cold fish. I wasn't living life, I was programming it. How could that be called love.

Another time, we were in the basement and he was being particularly sarcastic. I told him he was just plain mean. He told me this wasn't mean, to ask his ex-wife what mean was. She knew. He said that after their second child was born, they decided they wouldn't have anymore children. She got pregnant. He said that he took a gun that was in the house and held it to her head and told her, "Let's end this right now." He laughed, then told me, of course, she didn't know the gun wasn't loaded.

I was stunned! This was the man all the women thought was the perfect man, including me. When I confided in a friend as to how things were in my marriage, she told me to never mind telling anyone else because of his public persona. No one would believe me.

It wasn't too much later that I graduated from college with a Business Administration Degree. My pictures taken at that time show how haggard I looked.

I knew our marriage was in trouble and I sought outside help. I asked my husband if he would go to a counselor with me. To my astonishment, he said he would. I felt maybe we had a chance to work things out.

I had gone to a counselor after my second marriage ended to find out what my part was in the failures of two marriages. He told me, for one thing, I just cut things off. Why do I do that? I told him I didn't know. Why did he think I did that?

At another session, he suddenly said to me, "You're analyzing me and I don't know what to do about it." I realized I had been. On the drive home, I thought if I were analyzing him and he didn't know what to do about it, how could he help me with my problem? I didn't go back.

Against a friends advice (the woman who loaned me the $3,000 dollars) I signed myself into a private hospital for observation. I wanted an answer as to why I had married and divorced two times. I did not want to go through that again.

After I was in the hospital, I was told the psychiatrist had ordered an electric shock treatment for the next morning. A woman I knew had had nine treatments, but it was too soon to see results. My treatment was done. I was told that night there would be another treatment the next morning.

The more I thought about it the less sure I was I wanted another one. I wanted to be talked to, not zapped. I wanted help in figuring things out—being conscious at the time it was being discussed.

The next morning the orderlies came into my room to prepare me for the treatment. I told them my decision not to have it done. They said all right and proceeded to give me a shot.

They did that the last time, so I was aware they planned to go ahead.

I felt myself getting groggy, but was determined to keep enough sense to me to say I didn't want this. The psychiatrist came to stand by my head and I told him my decision. He tried to persuade me it was necessary. I kept repeating, "No."

He was upset with me and asked me who the doctor was here. I said, "You and I don't want it done." He gave the orders to get me out of there.

I called my friend and asked if she would come and pick me up. She came immediately and stayed with me for awhile.

Now, here I was again trying to find an answer so this marriage could be saved. The counselor saw us together, saw us separately, then together for 10 sessions. We learned some things, but not enough.

My husband wanted a brand new truck. He got one. We were sitting in lawn chairs on the side yard when he starting talking that all he had was a truck, while I had a house. I reminded him that I had the house before I knew him and the fact that he had just bought a new truck.

"That doesn't compare to having a house," he argued. Dawn came up on my horizon and I asked, "Are you saying your name should be on the deed for the house?" His answer was, "Have I earned it yet?" I asked him what that meant and he got upset and said, "Evidently, I haven't yet." It was left at that. I had mentioned, at other times, did he want his name on the deed? And he always said, "Not yet."

We slept in the downstairs bedroom. I was awaken one night because my husband's hand was lightly around my throat. I became scared and went to sleep in an upstairs bedroom. I didn't sleep for many nights. I thought he might come upstairs. He didn't.

I continued to sleep upstairs. Why didn't I call the police? Because I didn't have a job and I would lose my home, and I still had one child at home, though she was a teenager. I honestly thought things would just go on the way it was.

The septic system lines had never been filled in, so when I wasn't working in the shop, I was shoveling stone into the drainage ditches, laying 10- foot long plastic pipe, putting adhesive on parts that sealed two sections together. I shoveled in more stone, laid hay on top of the stone, and finally shoveled dirt back into 75- foot long ditches. While, I was doing this was when I learned yellow jackets built nests in dirt. I had to take care of that situation before I could continue. My husband stayed in the house, sitting at the kitchen table, doing crossword puzzles until it was time for him to go into work. He did come out one day, briefly.

* * *

He said he had been called into work this one afternoon for the night shift. He was a paid firefighter and this would happen fairly often. I had a late customer who asked me a question I couldn't answer. I told him I would get the answer for him and call him. I drove to the small station where my husband said he would be to see if he knew the answer. It was on the back side of dusk, so I couldn't see the guys too well in the room where they were watching television. I asked to speak to my husband. One of the guys told me he wasn't there. I told him my husband had told me this was where he would be. I thought they were joking with me.

He repeated that he wasn't there. I knew. I went home. I sat, wide awake, all night in the living room waiting for morning. He came home at the time he would have regularly come home if he had actually been working. I told him I had gone to the station and asked where he had been all night.

"I was at my girlfriend's," was his answer.

I suspected that was what it was, but was still stunned when he said it. I never questioned his work schedule.

I asked him to stay to give me time to get the business to where it would support me. He didn't want the business he said, and to me, that indicated he would give me the time I needed. A week later he moved out. Shortly after, I got the notice that divorce papers had been filed.

My whole emotional system shut down. I went on automatic pilot.

He came to the house to get his clothes and a few tools that were his. Everything else in the house had been there before we were married. I was awarded $75 a week for three years and at the end of three years, I was to pay him $75 a month for his VESTED INTEREST IN THE BUSINESS!

When he left, the business was bringing in almost $10,000 a year. The first year, after he was gone, it brought in a $1,000 less. The third year, it brought in almost $7,000. It became real clear if I wanted to keep my home, I had to get my act together and there was no guarantee of success.

THE LAST YEARS AT
AKRON ROAD

I read the manual and learned how to sharpen carbide tipped circular saw blades, drill bits, and router bits. One type of carbide tip is called triple chip. It had to be sharpened differently from a regular tip. There was a bevel put on each side of the tip, flat across the top of the tip with the face of the tip last. When you came toward the face with the diamond wheel, you had to back off at just the right moment or the tip would be rounded and would not cut correctly.

A new customer came into the shop with a 60- toothed triple chip carbide circular saw blade. He had taken it to a well established sharpening company to be sharpened and it wouldn't cut as it should. Would I see if I could salvage it?

I hadn't done such a blade. I told him I would see what I could do, no guarantee. I read the manual again, going step by step. I called him. He came and picked up the blade. He called the next day letting me know the blade worked perfectly. That gave my self-confidence a big boost.

Although, I was scared of the blow torch, I felt I would give it a try and conquer my fear, allowing me to put on new carbide tips myself. My son-in-law explained to me how the operating of the torch went. You turn this valve on first, then the other valve. When you turn the torch off you do it the opposite way.

I did both valves, then used the striker to get a flame, and boy did I get a flame. I slowly turned each valve until I got the color blue that was needed to do the job. My whole body was shaking and I turned the torch off. I tried it again with the same results and accepted I could not do this. People were telling me how women did it during the war and were still doing it. I felt like a total wimp. I knew if the business was to grow I needed to give this service. I asked my son-in-law if he would consider doing it. He had a full-time job and a family, but because there weren't that many that needed putting on he agreed. God bless him. He also did car repair work for me, which was a great help.

The car was acting up and I was told it might need new spark plug wires. They looked in bad shape. I decided to give this a go. I bought new wires. A daughter came that day to give me encouragement. I laid the new wires on the side of the car and noticed they were of various lengths and thought, that should help. I would take one old wire off at a time and find a new wire closest to that length. I was aware the old wires would have stretched through usage. I got done and asked my daughter to start the engine. I stepped back because I didn't know what might happen. She did. It did. It ran as smooth as could be. Boy, was I happy. We did one collective sigh of relief and of accomplishment.

Four mornings each week I would drive to my pick-up points to pick up work to be sharpened. Mondays and Thursdays, I went in one direction from the shop and the Tuesdays and Fridays I went in the other direction. I drove over seventy miles each of those days and was back at the shop before it opened at 10 a.m. Monday's work was taken back on Thursday and Thursday's work was taken back on Monday. The same routine on the other two days of the week. The shop closed at five weekdays and Saturdays at noon.

Twice, in all the years I was operating the business alone, a man laid his blades on the table and when he found out I was the one doing the sharpening, he picked up his blades and walked out of the shop.

I didn't know so many people still used a regular handsaw. They were a big part of the business. I took the handles off, used an electric sander to get gunk and rust off, set the teeth so the saw would go through the wood smoothly, giving the right size cut, and then I would spray a silicone spray on it to help keep it from rusting again. The spray did not leave an oily film on the blade.

Many men were amazed at how good their saws looked and worked. Every sharpened item was wrapped in newspaper and taped shut. I remembered everyone's name and was pleasant 98 percent of the time. There were people who tried to get their work cut the second time free. I knew that, but I did not argue with them. I redid it. A couple times, I didn't.

One male customer came in one day and asked for his sharpened work. I took it from where I kept all completed work and handed it to him. He told me he had taken work to two other places the same day he brought work to me. They told him that it would be ready today. I was the only one who had the work done. My policy was, if I saw that something wouldn't be done when I told the customer, I called letting them know and letting them know when it would be ready for sure. It was appreciated.

Another surprise to me was the number of buzz saw blades that were brought in to be sharpened. I thought they had gone the same way as the dinosaur. The smallest size blade to come in was 28- inches in width. The average were 39- inches.

The first thing you do to a circular saw blade is to round it. There is a piece of equipment you put the blade on to slowly bring to a grindstone to tick each tooth until all the teeth are the same length. Then, you take the blade to another piece of equipment and set each tooth, one side one way and the other side the opposite way. Then, you sharpen it. You follow the same procedure for buzz saw blades.

As I have said, I am five-foot-two and those blades are bulky and heavy to handle, and to carry from one piece of equipment to another wasn't easy. You needed muscle and determination. A customer came in with work to be done who had been in before with a buzz saw. He told me he took it home, put it on the machine and turned it on.

He cranked up the speed and it ran as smooth as glass with no vibrations, nothing. He brought down the speed because if the blade got loose, it would have caused a lot of havoc. He just wanted to see how it would run. This was another time my self confidence got a boost. You really have to get the blades round and set right, putting the right bevel on each tooth according to whether it was a rip or cross-cut blade.

I had to turn down push reel mowers as I didn't have the right piece of equipment. I tried, a couple times to sharpen them using a double-cut file. I would work on the reel then take the mower outside and mow a spot in my yard, seeing where it might need more work. It wasn't satisfactory. A lot of people still use push mowers because they have small city lots or for trim, while some even for exercise. I was losing potential business.

I was looking in the daily local paper and weekly penny saver to see if any new sharpening services had started up when I noticed an ad for a reel lawn mower sharpening machine. I called about it. Reel mowers were the only item the man did and he felt he was too old to do it anymore. My daughter, son-in-law, their pick up truck, and I went to get it. He explained briefly how it worked and we loaded it into the truck. I had cleared a spot for it in the shop and we placed it there. I was excited about having another service I could offer my customers. I tried my own reel mower on it and couldn't get it totally right. I contacted Foley as that was the manufacturer and requested a manual, which they sent.

One obstacle for me was the fact the mower had to be lifted up quite a distance to get it in place, let alone getting it anchored to the position necessary to sharpen it correctly. I was in my later fifties, now. It would take me over an hour to do one mower, accompanied by a lot of frustration. Sharpening is an extremely time consuming work, no matter what you are sharpening.

Operating was a full-time business, but I also had a house to maintain, housework to do, plus my dreams for it.

I planted asparagus, rhubarb, and red raspberries in a spot in the backyard. Nothing grew there or very little did. The land was so low, it was too wet for the plants. This meant digging more drainage ditches. Three coming from one direction and one long one for them to tie into to carry the water away.

I dug a four-foot deep and four-foot wide dry well. I gathered stones from around the yard, putting them into the dry well until it was half full. I hooked up the white plastic pipes extending it to the center of the dry well, shoveling small stone in and then dirt to fill it up. The asparagus, rhubarb and red raspberries grew. Satisfaction reigned. Then I went on to the next project.

I wanted wooden beams on the ceilings in four downstairs rooms. Not plastic pre-made beams, but wood—pine wood. I took out a loan and bought as many sixteen-foot, six-inch wide boards as I needed to do the job.

The first thing I did was to take a craft carving tool and carve small gouges along the edge on two of the three boards I used for each beam. I used a table fork to put marks that looked like aged cracks in the wood, lightly hitting the boards with a hammer to look like bumped into marks. I used a maple stain to give the beams a colonial appearance. The object was to make the beams seem like they had been there for years.

I had purchased two-by-fours and they were to be nailed to the ceiling so the board beams could be attached to them to hold the beams in place. Sometimes, I would have to crawl around in an unfinished crawl space to find where the joist was located before driving a nail through the ceiling, so I could find it from below. They really did add to the decor of the house. I got a lot of compliments on how much it did for each room. I felt I earned each of the compliments.

Montgomery Ward let me charge a riding lawn mower. It cut mowing time from five hours to three. Some of that was doing trim work.

My children and their spouses had been blessing me with grandchildren over the years. I saw a great deal of them. My premise was, if there was a grandparent, that person should be involved in their grandchildren's lives. No matter, if you're a busy person or not. I can tell you from experience a grandparent is an important and needed part of a child's life.

At one time, I had an older Volkswagen Camp Mobile. I would let the children use it as a playhouse. It was a lot easier to haul wood, cement, roofing, bags of dirt and stuff in. I even hauled a love seat and occasional chair to a daughter and her family's place. I couldn't afford to have all this delivered and didn't feel I could ask son-in-laws to do it all the time.

The man next door came to the shop and asked if he could borrow my extension ladder. There was a dead tree that he wanted to put a rope around up high enough so it could be pulled down. He had, already, used a chain saw at the base of the tree. I told him, sure, it was fine with me. What I couldn't figure out was why he would want to cut down MY dead tree, but with a little thinking it came to me. He and his wife kept their lawn immaculate and it bugged the heck out of him to see that dead tree.

About 10 minutes later, he comes in and asks me if I would help him pull the tree down. I thought, why not? He instructed me to take hold of the rope behind him, and when the tree started to fall, to go to my right to get out of the way. I wondered who he thought would be first in flight. I knew.

* * *

One day, I was standing at the kitchen sink doing the dishes when I heard words spoken to me as clear as though someone was standing right next to me. "You have been looking for a father's love."

I had just received the answer to my question as to what my part was in my three marriages and divorces. I haven't remarried since. I have learned I don't need a man in my life to validate my womanhood. Significant wisdom has always come to me in this way. I truly believe it was the voice of God giving me discernment. I remember the date those words were spoken— October 10, 1984.

The Good Book says, in Proverbs, that we are not to blow our own horn and I adhered to that, but the idea did come to me that a little recognition wouldn't hurt. Foley, the maker of the equipment I used, published a company magazine. I was small potatoes as far as business was concerned, but a woman operating a sharpening shop was unique, I thought.

I wrote the company a letter. Quite some time went by and I hadn't heard from them. I guessed that I was wrong and forgot about it.

I did get a call from a company representative letting me know they would like to send someone to interview me and to take some pictures. Would that be all right? I assured them it would be. He came. Their magazine went to every state in our country and to some foreign countries. Talk about being excited!

I also got a letter from a convict in a prison telling me he had seen my picture and read the article about my having my own shop. He wanted to know if I would write back to him. He was coming up for parole soon and wanted to come and visit me. I was sorry for the man, but with all I had going on I didn't have any left over time for anyone or anything. I reasoned there must be a Baptist church in his area. I sent his letter to the local Baptist minister asking him to help this man. He had written he had no one that visited or wrote him. Over the years, those that did had stopped.

After the Foley publication had been distributed, I got calls from people who had read it. There were congratulations and requests for help in starting such a business themselves. I advised them as to what I knew.

One day, I found myself talking to the equipment, which was an eye opener to me. You can't carry on a conversation with a machine. Obviously, I needed someone living in my house with me and decided to go with what I know best—children, specifically, foster children. I realized I was living my life by rote. I felt like a robot, emotions not needed to do sharpening. I applied to become a foster parent. I was checked out on all levels and was approved to be a foster parent. It was a blessing. I took on someone else.

The business had become a two-person business, so I made the decision to hire someone part-time to operate the carbide part of the business. This would relieve me of a great deal of work and allow the sharpening of precision tools from local manufacturers. The price of that sharpening would pay for the part-time help and provide a profit. I had gotten calls from industries in regards to doing their work. As it was now, they had to send their work to a large city quite a distance from them, causing problems for them. If I could do it they would provide me with steady work.

I talked to some of my customers to find out if any of them might be interested or knew someone who might be. One man had been laid off from his job and had a wife and children. Pay would be on a percentage basis of income generated from this new service. I provided the equipment, supplies and utilities. A starting date was agreed on. I was, cautiously, optimistic.

He showed up late and wasn't that fast a mover, but I thought once he got into the work, and gained self confidence, things would change. The next day, he was on time. The next day, I had to call him at his home. He came in. We had a talk and he decided he didn't want to do this kind of work.

A few other men showed an interest at first, but at the end said no. I got the definite impression from some of them, having a woman for a boss didn't set too well with them. I brought a woman in as she told me she could do the work. What she wanted to do was RUN MY BUSINESS. That, of course, would not happen. I was back to square one. It was such frustration because I knew how much income was available, but I couldn't tap into it.

One thing I did know for sure was I could not run the shop by myself and maintain the quality of the work or service. I worked too hard and sacrificed too much to let that occur.

Again, I put out the word and again some men showed some interest. I could show them how, after the purchase price for the equipment had been paid off, the profit was 50 percent. They didn't dare to take the risk.

One man was definite about purchasing the business for his brother. He lived on Long Island and his brother lived in my area. You could tell the brother was a little slow, but his brother had confidence in his ability. They came to the shop, but the brother showed no enthusiasm and was noncommittal in his attitude. His brother tried to talk him into it because he wanted him to have something to do to keep him busy because he lived so far away and couldn't help him. Money was no object. They would get back to me. They didn't call.

There was one man who was very interested, asking questions and kept coming back with more questions. I even invited him to a backyard cookout as a leisurely climate to discuss business. There were the foster children with he and I eating, and talking.

My accountant and I met with him in my home to discuss the financial figures for the business. My accountant brought my tax returns with him for the past five years. He answered any and all questions that was asked of him. This went on for at least two months. At one meeting, he told me his bank told him it wasn't a good investment. I had offered to every person I had talked to about buying the business that the equipment could stay at my shop for six months if it would be of help to them, and that I would stay on as a non-paid consultant for the same six month period. It was a sweet deal but no one saw it that way.

I knew there was no way I could operate this business by myself. I had to make a decision that crushed my spirit. I would have to file for bankruptcy. I contacted a lawyer and the process began.

I had noticed my thinking was becoming blurred. I would stand and not move. I didn't know where to move to. I would just look around. I felt empty inside. I would sigh a lot.

I started talking to my customers, letting them know that on the first of December, the shop would no longer be in operation. I put a sign in the shop door window stating this fact. I told them where there were other shops. I was 60 and had no idea how I was going to make a living.

I sold off the equipment piece by piece and when the last bit of equipment was gone, I converted the shop back into the two-car garage.

I always was able to handle driving a car really well. I had a natural feel for it, but now I was having trouble backing out of the garage. I'd start and it seemed to veer toward the side of the door opening, so I'd pull back in, try again, and the same thing would happen. I would drive in as straight as could be, but when it came to backing out I would mess up.

Once the front bumper was touching the side of the opening, starting to pull a piece of wood off. I kept going. I assessed the damage when I got back and a couple whacks of the hammer fixed it. The next time, same thing, and I kept on going. I could tell more damage was done this time. I was able to repair it with a couple nails and the hammer. The odd thing was I knew what was happening to the side of the opening, but it didn't bother me. It was as though I was in another world and observing all this from a distance.

I sat on the back deck all day, day after day. I was barely functioning. I still had enough sense to recognize I had a problem—a serious problem. I reasoned it out that I was suffering from burn-out. It had to do with my emotions, so I didn't call the doctor, I made an appointment to see the minister. He counseled me. I believe I saw him three times. I thought it helped, but later I knew it hadn't that much. What was wrong was too deep.

I was in no condition to be a caring and effective foster parent. I contacted the Social Service office informing them of my decision to discontinue being a foster parent, effective immediately. The children had enough traumatic life experiences that they deserved and needed their foster parent to provide the stability, nurturing and direction necessary to enable them to live a fulfilling and productive adult life. I couldn't do that. I felt so sad. I felt so empty.

I was able to sell my home for enough to payoff the mortgage and had $5,000 left. My car I was driving was an eight-cylinder, old, and needed many repairs. I purchased a small four-cylinder Dodge Omni, for $3,000. What was left was for relocation purposes.

I packed my entire belongings and my family came with their pick up trucks, moving my possessions to a daughter's barn and attic. What I didn't throw away, I gave away and was lucky to sell a few things. I moved into another daughter's apartment until I could find an apartment for myself. I lived in a house for so long the idea of living, permanently, in an apartment wasn't appealing. Beggars can't be choosers, right?

I had applied for an apartment in a low income housing complex. Sometimes that can take up to a year waiting for a vacancy, but mine took three weeks. These apartments are small and I was used to space. I was used to being able to step outside into my own yard and have privacy. I loved living in the country and now I lived in a city. I lived there for nine years, getting more and more depressed. I had one serious bout of clinical depression.

I'm not a coffee latch person. Never had the time to be one. It didn't interest me now. I needed some part of my former life to give meaning to this one. There was a bit of lawn between the building and the sidewalk. I enjoyed working with flowers. I wrote the office of the complex asking for permission to plant flowers in that space. They gave me the approval to do so. I used my old spading fork, digging up the sod, used a small tool to knock the sod off, and put the grass in the dumpster that was on the premises.

I purchased perennials, plus five rose bushes and some annuals plants. The money for this didn't come from a surplus of money, but from a need to get my hands in dirt—and possibly to give other residents a boost to their spirits. I got carried away as I dug up ground on both sides of the sidewalk that led from the front door to the parking lot and was about six feet wide. It helped. I didn't get in trouble, though.

Toward the end of my stay there, a gazebo was put on the grounds. The second Christmas season, I wrote another letter, this time for permission to put a live tree inside the gazebo. I was informed that I could. I bought the tree, decorations, lights, and the garland to go around the outside railing. Again, filling a need of mine and hoping to give the other residents a sense of Christmas joy.

I contacted a church that was across the street to see if their children's choirs could come and sing carols. Cookies and cocoa would be served afterwards. They agreed to sing.

Our entrance keys fit all the other entrance doors to the apartment buildings. I would let the carolers and their chaperones in each building. They would spread out and sing, ending with, "We Wish You A Merry Christmas." People came to their doors to listen and say, thank you. We all felt the joy.

* * *

I did this for four more years, but the last two years I got a tree and did the decorations. I was in my sixties and it would be bitter cold. There was also taking everything down. A couple times a grandson would come and help me put up the tree and decorate. They followed my directions. We enjoyed ourselves. The longing for the country never left me. The open space, the peace and quiet, the silent nights. Nature the only sound.

Someone I knew who was living in another low income apartment told me of a place close by that was at the edge of a small village. I was, initially, excited about the prospects of moving away from the city, then the thought of packing everything again seemed too much of an effort. My children thought it was a good idea and came to do most of the packing.

I had drove to the place and liked what I saw—fields on two sides of the complex. It wasn't right in the village and the village was on the shores of Lake Ontario. I also like the water. When an apartment opened up the pick up trucks came again. There were about fourteen of us and we made short work of that move. A couple daughters and granddaughters made sure my bed was set up, the sheets and blankets on, so when they left I could climb right in. They came back the next day to help.

The apartment was one floor, and the amenities were great, like a storage room, a pantry off the kitchen and a small PRIVATE PORCH! This is where I am and plan on staying.

This has been my journey as a foster child from start to end—which is today, for the moment, and will pick up tomorrow because you never completely get over being a foster child.

I have used my own words telling this journey, in my own way. I have not tried to make it artificially styled or grammatically correct. Commas and such have been placed where I thought a pause was needed. I did not do this to insult anyone's love of the English language. I wanted this to be true in all ways. You can make your own judgments on the issue of the foster child system.

I have let a few people read the manuscript and have varied responses. They ranged from the fact they wanted to get their hands on the people who are in charge and put them in jail for the rest of their lives, to they found it to be a little self serving.

My hope is, after you have read this book, you will come away with a better understanding of the foster child system, realizing the system needs some changes that make it more amendable to the children's circumstances and emotional needs.

MY FOSTER CHILDREN'S JOURNEY

What you will be reading are the true accounts of the foster children who made their home with me from three days to three years. You will gain insight into the foster parents role in the foster child system

Foster children and foster parents are the two most important parts of that system. The reality is that Social Services and the children's biological parents emerge as the most important part. Foster parents are designated the job of being holding centers and the foster children spend their time in limbo.

I can not, by law, use these children's birth names. I will be using a pseudo first name only.

Prepare yourselves for what you are about to read. Guard your heart.

DOUGLAS, JOSUHA, DAVID

The phone rang in the middle of the night. The person that called identified themselves as a police officer from the nearby city. She asked me if I would, possibly, consider taking three little boys into my home. She had called Social Services and gotten their approval to do so, and that she had called a number of foster parents and I was her last hope. I told her to bring them. This was my introduction into my second time as a foster parent.

The children were in the apartment all by themselves. A neighbor heard children crying and called the police. The apartment was a mess. The police didn't know where the mother was or when she would be home. The officer bundled the youngest in a blanket, as he was totally wet from top to bottom. She grabbed a few clothes, stopping at an all night store on the way to my home to get some diapers. There were none in the apartment.

Then, they were at my door. The scared look in their eyes broke my heart. In an emergency case like this, the children are with you for three days, giving Social Services time to sort out the situation and to make other arrangements.

The one year old, Douglas, was crying and calling for his mommy. I drew bath water and put all three children in the tub. They were dirty and had a foul odor about them. I washed their hair. A warm bath would help them to relax. I could tell the

130

oldest boy, David, was used to having the responsibility of his brothers. He was only four. My bedroom was on the first floor. I wanted the boys near me so I bedded them down on the two-piece sectional couch in the living room. They went to sleep.

I had my business and thought, beings this was only going to be a three day period, I could handle both. WRONG! I would set the boys up with easy puzzles, coloring books and crayons, children's books to look through, and set the television for cartoons, thinking I could do a little sharpening and check on the boys. I left the kitchen door open, so I could see into the kitchen and dining room. I would have to shoo Douglas back into the kitchen because he was determined to come into the shop. He just wanted to be with me. I knew that but it was a dangerous place for a child to be. I would have to wait on customers and then I couldn't see the boys.

On one of my check-on times, I stood open mouthed at what I saw. A full box of cereal had been emptied allover the living room carpet. I soon learned Joshua was the instigator of whatever happened. He was two.

Of course, I made them three meals a day. They ate as though they hadn't eaten in a week. Another time, after I had waited on a customer, then taken a look into the kitchen, I saw everything from the lower cupboards that didn't have a lock on it, scattered allover the kitchen floor. There was no way I could do the sharpening work and take care of three little boys. I called customers, pushing ahead their pick-up day. The new work that came in had to be given a later pick-up day. Some were not pleased.

The third day came and went and I hadn't heard a word from Social Services. Early in the morning, I called and explained my situation. It wasn't as though they didn't know I had my own business. The business was my source of income.

They were not pleased by my phone call. I got the feeling they thought I was being selfish. After all, I wanted to be a foster parent because I care about children. The business was my source of income! It had nothing to do with not caring about children. If I couldn't make the mortgage payments there wouldn't be a foster home to bring children to. On about the fifth day the boys were with me, Social Services came and picked them up. They were taken back to their mother's apartment. They were giving her one more chance.

Foster parents do receive a certain monthly payment when foster children are placed in their home. This helps to cover the extra costs of food, utilities, laundry soap, water, toilet items, personal hygiene, and such. The foster parents I knew would buy the children extras all the time with no asking for reimbursement. If they had children of their own, the foster children received whatever their own did.

You don't discriminate between children. That would be totally wrong. Unthinkable. I know what that would do to a foster child's feelings of self- worth. They have little to begin with and some have none.

There was another call from the police, could they bring a five-year-old boy to my home. Someone had reported seeing this child walking the city streets at daybreak, all by himself. It was Sunday. It was winter. He had no shoes or jacket. He was a thin blonde boy. Quiet.

I couldn't understand what he was saying, too well. He and I got into my car, went to a store, and I bought him a pair of sneakers. A daughter brought one of her kids' jackets for him to wear. Social Services had the situation handled in three days.

His mother had gone out for the evening, leaving the boy with a couple, saying she would be back for him at 10. When the couple got up the next morning and saw that he was still there, they got mad at the mother for not keeping her word. They turned the boy out onto the street. He told the case worker he was trying to find his way home. The mother was given another chance.

SYBIL

The first non-emergency child to be brought to my home was a fourteen-year-old girl. A fourteen-year-old girl gave me feelings of apprehension, but I didn't become a foster parent to be selective of what child I would take into my home. All children were welcome.

She was petite, slender, and had blonde streaks in her hair— very pretty and knew it, a flirt who wore sexy clothes.

I was told she ran away from her parents home, frequently. Her parents didn't feel they could cope with these actions anymore. She became a ward of the court.

The school bus came at 7:15. Sybil started getting ready at four o'clock. I set my alarm for six. I was awaken by a pan being banged onto a stove burner, the refrigerator being opened and closed a number of times. I got up. My belief is the parent is supposed to be up before the children in the morning.

She had gotten the items out for a fried egg and a glass of milk, which she warmed, and made toast. I fixed it for her. She said she did it at home. You learn, after having a couple foster children in your home, they expect to do things the way it was done at home and don't see why it shouldn't continue to be so in the foster home.

I asked Sybil why she got up so early and her answer was to get ready for school. I pointed out what time it was and she said it took her that long and it did. She would change what she was wearing many times, apply makeup that had to be perfect before

133

starting the time consuming part of the whole morning, which was fixing her hair. She would comb and tease, comb and tease until she felt it was the way she wanted it. It was very bouffant. She did look great as she went out the door.

After a week of my getting up at four and fixing her breakfast, then sitting at the kitchen table waiting until the time for her to get on the bus, I set my alarm for six. I could see the kitchen from my bedroom and was right there in case a problem occurred.

She fixed her own breakfast then, making a terrible mess. She made cocoa and it would boil over because she was upstairs doing whatever, come racing downstairs when she smelled burnt milk, eggs would splatter over everything, and toast would burn. She always was truly sorry, but I couldn't seem to get it through to her that you are supposed to stay in the kitchen when you're cooking.

The fact that bugged me was that I was the one left with the mess to clean up. I solved that problem. I told her the mess would still be there when she got home from school and she was to clean it.

The children had chores that were to be done each weekend. Things like changing the sheets on their bed, dusting, running the vacuum, learning how to sort their dirty cloths and do their laundry. They set the table every night for supper, taking turns to do the dishes. They needed to learn how to do these things for when they were on their own.

Homework was done at the kitchen table. I monitored the TV programs they watched and how much of their time could be spent watching TV. I had quite a few videos. I was a movie buff. Over the years of them watching the videos it became evident the favorite one was *The Color Purple*. Sybil found all this togetherness boring.

She asked me, after school one day, if she could go to the

library to study with her friends They needed to look up some things for a certain class. I was uneasy about this, but felt I should show her I was trusting her. I drove her to the library with the promise that someone's parent would have her home by eight. Eight came and went. I gave her another fifteen minutes and then told the other foster child, who had recently come, to get in the car.

We went into the library and walked around until I saw her. I went up to her and told her she was to come home with me. She starting yelling and cursing at me, using the infamous four letter word.

I put my hand around her arm to help her stand up and she told me to get my goddamned hands off her. I calmly insisted she was to come with me. She kept yelling and finally did get up and start for the front door. She veered to the left, starting down to the bottom floor of the library. I went further down, turned to face her, and told her to go to the car. A woman clerk came from the bottom floor, asking what was going on? I told her things were under control and she left. I was surprised when Sybil actually did turn to leave.

When we got outside, she sneered at me, "How can I go to the car if I don't know where it is?"

I showed her where it was parked. She went to it. I unlocked the doors and she got in. I had turned on the ignition when she yelled at me, "Why did you ask for a fourteen-year-old girl if you can't handle it." I yelled back, "I didn't."

I heard her lean back against the seat and she didn't say another word on the way home. Myself, I was a quivering mess inside.

Her birth father, who was divorced from her mother, started coming to the house. Anyone visiting a foster child has to get prior approval from Social Services and they are to come only at the stated times. He did that for a couple times, then started showing up unexpectedly, saying it was the only time he could get a ride out here.

The first time I let him in. The second time, I didn't. He sweet talked to me like I was one of God's angels for taking his daughter into my home. It didn't work. Sybil was upset at me. She said I was mean. You could see how much she needed a father.

He hadn't been coming to see Sybil for quite some time, so she believed he had changed, that he really wanted to be with her now. He loved her. These children need to believe this.

He spent a lot of time talking to me when he was here. Foster parents are to be close by when relatives visit because, to be honest, you don't know what might be happening in your home or what plans that are being made that wouldn't be to the best interest of the foster child. He was trying to talk me into going in business with him, raising some kind of moth. It was rare. He would call during the week and talk to Sybil. She was trusting him more and more. I kept Social Services in-formed of all visits and phone calls.

One morning, I became aware I hadn't heard Sybil performing her daily routine and got up. I heard nothing, thinking she had finally overslept. I went to her bedroom. Her bed was made and a sheet of paper leaned against the pillow. I knew then that she had run away. I sat on her bed and silent tears began to express my sorrow.

Somehow, I had messed up big time or she wouldn't have run away. I took the paper and read that it wasn't my fault. She was so mixed up and needed to get away from everyone to find out who she was. I remember thinking that was what I was trying to help her with.

I called her case worker. I told her I remembered Sybil telling me that her father had told her he was going to move to Florida because there was a lot of work there. When he got a place to live and enough money so he could afford to take care of her, he would ask Social Services to allow her to live with him. She contacted the police and they told the case worker they had a warrant out on him and wanted to know where he lived. No one knew.

It didn't surprise me when he called that night asking to speak to Sybil. I told him she wasn't home. He wanted to know where she was and when would she be getting home. It clicked! She was with him and he was doing this to throw people off base. I told him what I thought and, of course, he denied it. I told him there was a warrant out for him and he better get her back to my home fast. He was in enough trouble with the law as it was.

Again, he denied she was with him. I had heard him talking to some female and I knew it wasn't Sybil. Within fifteen minutes, Sybil was walking in the kitchen door. He had dropped her off at the intersection a few feet from the house.

Sybil told me that the last time they had talked, he had convinced her to meet him out front of the house later that night. They went to a motel in the city about five miles away. They were going to Florida.

The woman, with her father, was nice to her. Her father, after awhile, made moves toward Sybil that she felt wasn't right. It broke her heart. He left the motel room to make the phone call to me, telling her he was going to throw me off guard and that they would be safe. When he came back he told her to get in the car. I hadn't been fooled. Do you have any idea what this episode did to this young girls emotions? Devastation. I called the case worker and told her he was at some motel in the city.

There was another incident before this one that didn't help Sybil's sense of self worth. She asked me if she could go to a girlfriend's house for awhile. Some of her other girlfriends were going to be there. I called the home, talked to the mom and was assured what she had said was true. I gave a deadline of eleven o'clock. She didn't come home. I called the girl's home. The mother told me that the girls had gone to someone else's house.

Number, please. I made the call and the noise was ear busting. I asked for Sybil. She wasn't there. Where is she? I don't know. Who is this? The phone disconnected. It was now 12:30. I didn't know what to do. I didn't want to call her case worker and take the chance they would put her in a juvenile detention place. I was sure that would be what happen.

I stood in the dark of the living room, looking out the front window. Where was she? Maybe she would call me to come and get her. She had before.

I stood there all night. I gave myself until morning for her to come back before I put in that call to her case worker. It started to become daylight. It was very foggy. I thought I saw a movement to my right and kept looking. I saw her walking along the road headed for the house. My mind raced as to how I should handle this. Disciplinary action was definitely necessary.

I walked toward the kitchen door, wondering how to greet her. With admonishment? Before I had a plan formulated—we were standing face to face and I threw my arms around her, saying, "I'm so glad you're home." We both cried.

Social Services decided Sybil wasn't foster child material. They put plans into motion to place her in an institution. It was done. I felt them to be wrong with their decision. I went past just missing her. We kept in contact for awhile. She would earn and lose privileges, then get them back.

Later, when another foster child had been placed with me, we were taken on a tour of the high school that she would be attending. I heard a female voice call my name and when I turned toward the voice it was Sybil. I was so happy to see her.

She told me she would be graduating that year. How about that? Her plan was to join the Navy. Another time, I saw her and her mother in a store. She had a full-time job. We chatted for awhile.

I heard she was going to be married to someone. I haven't heard anything since then. I hope, with all my heart, she is doing well and happy. Would I like to know how things are with her, sure, but that is part of being a foster parent. These children aren't yours, but you feel like they are. Sometimes, the line gets blurred within yourself. I found it happened often, like every time.

LILLIAN

This was an extremely difficult placement. I've never seen such an angry child. All the time, angry. She was 10 years old, very tall, very thin, with short blondish hair.

I asked the parents of two of my grandchildren if they could come to my home and stay a couple days. They were the same age as Lillian. I thought this would help her ease into a new home, where she would be staying for awhile. My granddaughters agreed to the plan. They came the night before Lillian was to arrive. The girls asked me the next evening if they could leave. They couldn't handle Lillian's hostile attitude.

Sybil was still in my home when Lillian was brought by her case worker. There were times when she acted as an older sister to our new member. Lillian showed some positive response back to her.

Lillian had an older sister and two younger siblings. Each child lived in a separate foster home. One Social Services rule, now, is to keep siblings together. In this case that was not an option. They acted out when they were together, which was one of the primary reasons they were placed in foster care. All of the children had been sexually abused by a relative.

Their parents were borderline retarded. The father was mentally unstable, which was my understanding from what had been told to me. The mother was a warm hearted woman who didn't understand parenting. Social Services provided sessions of parenting skills to the parents, in their home, in hope they would learn enough to be able to have their children returned to them. One question that was posed to them gave them their answer.

When the perpetrator of the sexual abuse was released from jail, would they allow him into their home? The answer was, yes. Why? Because he is family and you don't keep family from your home. Shortly after, Social Services went to court to have the parental rights taken away. The children were now permanent wards of the court.

I now had two more children making their home with me. A four year old boy and a ten year old girl. Lillian was always lying to get these children in trouble.

There were three upstairs bedrooms. Each child had their own room. I noticed the boy was acting different than how he acted normally. I would talk to him, casually bringing into our conversation that I thought he wasn't feeling well, that he looked sad. You have to be careful how you try to get information from a child when you think something is wrong. You don't want to pose a question, in a way, that will get an answer they think you want.

It eventually came out that Lillian was coming to his bed and would lie down on top of him. His take on this was that he couldn't breath and it scared him. He said he would ask her to get off of him.

I spoke to Lillian and she denied it. I told her that I knew it to be true and it was not to happen again. If it did, there would be action taken, possibly removal from my home. She didn't want to leave. I didn't go to bed until late each night. I would sit on the steps going upstairs for many nights listening for what I hoped would be silence. After two weeks, I stopped because I was sure she had taken me seriously. It never did happen again, but you always have it on your mind. The little boy got adopted.

The children went to Sunday school. I would receive reports of Lillian's bad behavior. She joined Girl Scouts. Same reports...very disruptive at meetings, didn't want to do badge requirements, wouldn't help at service projects. I removed her from the organization. It wasn't fair to the girls who were working to accomplish their goals.

She went to a church camp for one week. After the girls had gotten back home, I got a call from one of the girl's mother. She wanted to know if Lillian had brought a small pillow home from camp. It had a horse's head on the front and it belonged to her daughter, who had shared the same cabin with Lillian. The mother told me it was common knowledge that Lillian would go off, by herself, into the woods that were next to the cabins. I told her I would ask, plus search the house to see if I could find it. I asked and I looked. The answer to both efforts was negative.

Lillian had done a lot of talking about the pillow when she got home, and I suspected she had done something with it. All the other mothers called had said there was no pillow at their place. I believe Lillian wanted that pillow very much—and knowing she couldn't have it, hid it in the woods.

I had a birthday party for Lillian at my oldest daughter's home. They lived in the country and had a lot of land so the guests could have a grand time. The guests were my children and their children, quite a few, actually. There was a birthday cake, singing and presents. Music was played on the radio and my son-in-law danced with her. It was a great party and she seemed to enjoy being the center of attention.

Melinda, who was nine, and Lillian didn't hit it off from the start. Melinda was short and small boned. That wasn't the problem. I found out what it was later, in a very dramatic way.

The girls had been outdoors playing before coming inside. Lillian had something very important to tell me. They had been running and both fell down, with Lillian landing on top of Melinda. Melinda had said that it felt like the S-word. Lillian said that, of course, we knew what that meant.

I asked Melinda to come into my bedroom with me and we sat on my bed. I talked about what was said and asked for her version. It was the same. She told me that things had happened to her at home. It was her father. She appeared to have a sense of relief to rid herself of this horrible secret. I called her case worker and action was taken that day. That will all be explained when I relate Melinda's story.

Each child has their own counselor, going once a week to see them. I would take them and stay in the waiting room until they were done with their session. During the week, I would write down every nuance of the children's daily actions and words, sending the information to the counselor, so they would have my report before the children came in to see them for their regular appointment.

I explained in the letter that this was not me finding fault with the children. I was sending every-thing to them, so they, with their training, could pick out the wheat from the chaff. A counselor called one of the case workers, telling her what I was doing and how much help it was. The case worker called me, wondering why she wasn't getting a report. She did from then on.

* * *

The two girls and myself went to Bruce's adoptive home to visit him and have a cookout. There was an above ground swimming pool on the premises and all three children were swimming. Bruce got chilled and got out of the pool, wrapping himself with a large towel. All of a sudden, a friend of the

143

adoptive mother yelled, "Let her up!"

We couldn't see Melinda. Lillian had her hand on Melinda's head, holding her under water. We moved. She let go. I had the girls get out of the pool and we went home.

I questioned Lillian about her actions and her answer was 'we were fooling around.'

I understood Lillian by now and knew that was the wrong answer. I knew, without a doubt, she had been trying to drown Melinda. It shook me to my core. I had never experienced anything like this in my entire life. I contacted her case worker.

An appointment was set up with a psychiatrist for Lillian. Her office was in a very large city about an hour's drive away. I rode to the appointments with her and the case worker.

There were probably four meetings, all together spaced every couple of weeks. The psychiatrist said, at our last meeting, she was sure Lillian wouldn't do any physical harm to herself or anyone else. She discharged her as a patient.

When we got outside, walking toward the car, I turned to the case worker and said, "Yes, she will."

I was proven right. The foster parent knows these children in their home better than anyone, but they aren't listened too. We don't have a degree. What we have is common sense and intuition. That really used to upset me because they wouldn't take what I said seriously.

One evening, after supper, the girls were washing and drying the supper dishes. Lillian was doing the washing and Melinda the drying. I was in the living room watching the local news. The girls came rushing into the room with Lillian telling me Melinda had stabbed herself in the arm. There were small pricks along her right arm with a fairly deep cut in her upper arm. The doctor took care of the wounds. Then, Melinda was in the hot seat of attention.

Something was wrong with this picture, but I couldn't figure what it was. Finally, after going over it in my mind a few times, I got it. Lillian had been standing on Melinda's right side. Melinda was right handed, it would have been almost impossible, for Melinda to stab herself with her left hand, particularly with Lillian standing right beside her. I was sure.

Melinda wasn't home, so I took advantage of that time to talk to Lillian. I started discussing the incident. She talked freely about it. I casually laid it out that I just, couldn't see how Melinda had stabbed herself and, then, I asked her, "Do you have something you want to tell me?"

She admitted that she had stabbed Melinda. When I asked why, she told me that she was jealous of Melinda sharing any of my time. She wanted me all to herself. Case worker.

The decision was made that she should be placed in an institution where there was constant supervision and a no nonsense attitude on the part of the staff. She was there a few years. We communicated. She invited me to a chorus concert she was singing in, where she was living.

There, also, was a young woman around 27 seven years of age, that Lillian had known a few years back. She had been a foster child in this woman's parents' home.

I had been told they requested she be removed from their home after a three week period. They had her removed because of her behavior. Lillian would hear from her, occasionally. It was this young woman who would play a pivotal part in Lillian's life.

She began to come to my home to visit Lillian. She had approval from the case worker. She would take her out to eat, visit with the woman's parents, and such. Once, they went to a riding stable, rented two horses, and followed the trails set up by the stable. Lillian enjoyed that, very much.

The young woman, I'll call her Jane, told me at a later date that she was considering adopting Lillian. I had considered this myself, once. She needed stability in her life, continuity. She needed to know someone wanted her for their own. I never mentioned this to Lillian because I had a lot of thinking to do before I approached her with the idea. It had to be a mutual decision. I was in my mid-fifties at the time.

I knew Lillian's problems wouldn't just go away because I adopted her. And I wasn't sure, as I got older, if I could handle things. Then, I wondered if it would be fair to Lillian because I would not have the energy or stamina to give her as active of a life she deserved as a young person. I decided against it.

I wasn't sure Jane was the right person. Not from jealously, I thought her rather immature. I called the case worker as to Jane's intentions. She was delighted. The process began.

In New York, at this period of time, the process was a series of visits at the prospective parent's home, which in this case was an apartment in the large nearby city.

It starts with a one day visit, progresses to an overnight, and then a stay over for a weekend. This gave both parties the opportunity, close up, as to their compatibility. If all goes well, the child moves into the home for a six-month period. If that works out, then legal adoption proceedings begin. I believe this to be an excellent program.

The day before Lillian was to leave my home to move to Jane's residence, she asked me the same question that Bruce had, "Will you still be my grandma?"

I assured I would. One event that I found unsettling when the visitations were still going on was something Lillian told me. Jane had a boyfriend and she had asked Lillian's case worker if it would be all right for him to move in with them, permanently. The case worker gave her approval.

I was shocked by that decision. What about teaching morals

to Lillian. She had sexual problems to begin with. Then, my thinking went to anything is all right if it gets a child off the welfare rolls. What's best should come before someone's love life in this circumstance. Here, at one time, I had been told to cover up the sump pump opening more because a child might fall in. The opening was only three inches larger then the sump pump, and no child could possibly fall in, yet they okayed immorality. They lost my respect.

I would get phone calls from Lillian in the early evening or late evening telling me she was alone and scared. Jane was visiting friends. Lillian was to call if there was a problem. This happened quite often.

Lillian would call the police on Jane. Jane would call me and tell me how bad Lillian was be- having. I'm sure she was aware Lillian was calling me. Jane said to me that she didn't think she should have to give up her previous way of living because Lillian was there.

I could tell she didn't grasp just what the responsibilities of being a parent were. She told me they were in a public city park once and the police showed up. Lillian told me she had to do all the housework. Jane told me she did nothing. I was trying to help this to work out and becoming highly anxious.

I tried explaining to Jane that she wasn't aware of what her part was in this relationship. Eventually, I called the case worker because it was not my place to be an arbitrator, nor did I have the authority to do so. Jane made the decision as six months was at hand that she wouldn't adopt Lillian. When she got this news, I was so concerned for Lillian, rejected again. How could she possibly cope with this.

It took me back to the time when she asked me if I would still be her grandma and the look on her face, the glow in her eyes. She was happy. This was the first and only time I had ever seen a normal emotion from her. She was a child with good news. She was ready to bloom as a person. Pure joy came from her. I was frightened for her, now.

I received a phone call from her case worker asking me if I would take Lillian back into my home, while plans were being made as to what to do next. I said I would. There was another foster child in my home by then.

Lillian told the case worker that I did not want her back. She wouldn't believe it. In about four days, she did and was brought to my home. This was not the girl that left my home. She was different.

Cold, hard, emotionless, and nonparticipating. Her contact with the other foster girl was nominal.

She was taken to an institution. She was there a couple years, contacted an aunt, and had her come and get her, and she was gone. She lived in my area with her aunt. She called to say she and her aunt had a big argument and she had moved out.

At Christmas season, I kept calling the phone number she had given me to let her know I would be bringing presents to her, but got no answer. I drove to the place, knocked, and with no answer, I left the bag hanging on the door knob. After I got home, I thought what a stupid thing to do and drove back. It was gone. It was awhile before she got back to me letting me know she had gotten the presents.

She and a boyfriend had moved in together in a different apartment. I invited them to my place for a roast beef dinner. They accepted. He was a nice young man, good manners, interesting conversation. When they left, he invited me to their place for a spaghetti dinner sometime.

We set a date. I looked forward to it. He planned and cooked the entire meal. Lillian's mother came after awhile. I was surprised when Jane showed up. She told us how she had told her friends how happy she was that she was going to her kids' home for the first time and to eat dinner.

I conversed with everyone. She didn't. She talked mainly to Lillian. When we were finished eating, I stayed for a little bit, then put on my coat to leave. I looked back at the table and saw Lillian standing beside Jane with her arm around her shoulders, just staring at me. Jane had a smile. I got the message.

The only time I heard from Lillian after that was when she wanted something. She had chosen money and position. I accepted it. We do not contact each other anymore.

BRUCE

Bruce came to make his home with me when he was four. He had blonde hair, blue eyes, and an attitude. He had been sexually abused by his mother. He constantly sassed, threw temper tantrums, did what he KNEW he shouldn't do, and picked on the other foster children even though they were larger as he continually tried to get them in trouble. His middle name became, Discipline.

I was, at least, his third foster parent since placement. By the time he went to bed, he was exhausted. So was I. His parents were borderline retarded. Bruce wasn't. He had a mixed race, older brother.

What I had noticed about the children was how much they ate. They started to fill out and grow taller. Their skin color changed from very pale to a healthy pink. Structure slowly brought about emotional changes. Definite times for meals, bedtime, regular bath times, work times, play times, manners taught, compassion taught, discipline meted out when told it would be. They knew what to expect and it didn't change from one day to the next. They had a sense of security, probably, for the first time in their life.

Bruce was one of my fortunate foster children. When he was five, a single woman made it known she would like to adopt him. She already knew him from a program she worked in as an instructor. She would visit him on occasions at my home.

Social Services started the process for adoption. He would

visit for a day, then an overnight, then a weekend to assess how both parties got along. I could tell he was scared at first, but he wouldn't show it. By that time, we had bonded and I could feel what he was feeling. He reverted back to doing and saying the right thing, what he thought everyone wanted to see and hear. He shut his feelings down, something I could totally relate to.

The day to move was tomorrow. I was happy for him, but sad within myself, for me. You do get attached. At bedtime he looked at me and in a low, quivering voice asked me, "Will you still be my grandma?" Tears blurred my vision as I gave him a hug and said, "Yes, I will always be your grandma." This is something foster parents have to learn to deal with. These are not our children and believe me it is not always easy to let go, but for everyone's sake we must.

I am so happy to report I still am Bruce's grandma. We see each other every year. I send him birthday and Christmas cards. The three of us go out to eat, at least once a year, usually during the Christmas season. I go to their home. Bruce is active in their church.

The youth group went to Mexico a couple years ago and he brought home a poncho for me. I am extremely proud of the person he has become. The woman who is Bruce's adoptive mom is the very best person for this honored role in his life. I truly believe she was sent by God.

MELINDA

She was nine when she came to me. A petite, long haired blonde, large blue eyes, very quiet, with a sexual aura to her.

She was easily lead by Lillian. I believe she was afraid of her. Her moments of giddiness were inappropriate for the situation. Lillian would ask her why she was laughing and Melinda would answer that she didn't know.

One summer morning, Lillian and Melinda were playing in the backyard, and after awhile they came into the house with Lillian saying she had something to tell me. They had been running around and they fell to the ground with Lillian landing on top of Melinda. She reported, "Melinda said this feels like the S-word." Lillian said, "We know what the S-word is." My thoughts were—we have a problem.

I asked Melinda if she had said that. She was to tell the truth. She wouldn't get in trouble. She slowly nodded her head. She and I went into my bedroom where we could talk privately. I told her that I would like to know how she knew about the S-word, again reassuring her she was not and would not be in trouble. I needed to know. She explained. It was her father. I could see what a burden it took off her, now that she was free of the secret. I held her while we sat on my bed. I told her I had to call her case worker to let her know what was just found out. Did she understand that I did? Again, a slow nod of her head. Things happened fast.

She was taken for an internal examination which proved

what she told me. I wanted to go with her because I sensed she needed someone there who cared about her. I wasn't allowed too. She was interrogated by a police officer and she was brought home to me. She was so closed in emotionally that I couldn't tell exactly how all of this affected her. In a case like this, you hug the child and continue the regular routine of living, giving the child a sense of continuity. The world wasn't going to come to an end. There would be a tomorrow. They were safe.

Her parents were borderline retarded. They were brought in for questioning. The father denied the charges. I was told he passed the lie detector test because he was in total denial within himself that he could have done such a thing. Which meant he couldn't be charged with anything. I am vague on what took place next as I was traumatized by what Melinda was going through, how this would affect her teenage years, her adult relationships. Slowly, I leveled out.

Parental visitations were limited for awhile. Melinda couldn't see her father at all. Of course, she wanted to as he was her father and she loved him. She couldn't see the ramifications of the situation. She, eventually, did.

As with all foster children, at least all the ones I know about, go to counseling sessions with licensed counselors. I would go with Melinda. Sometimes, she met with the counselor alone, sometimes I did and sometimes there would be the three of us.

I was very impressed by her counselor. I could tell she knew her field of expertise. Even with that she could get Melinda to open up just so much. The look in Melinda's eyes was one of determination. She played a game of cute coyness to throw her counselor off from her intent. She was clever. She was loyal to her parents, no matter what.

The counselor had a set of dolls representing a family and would set up scenes for Melinda to play-act through. She would go along with it up to a point, giving nothing useful away. She was aware of what was wanted from her and she wasn't going to reveal anything significant. We were both concerned about not learning anything in depth. We knew it was only a mater of time before visits with her father were allowed. The parents, also, had counseling sessions with Melinda's counselor. The mother did not exert her opinions.

When I heard this I wasn't surprised because of an incident that happened at my house. It was on a day when the mother was coming for her visit, alone, and was involved in an accident right in front of my house. She was turning into the driveway when her car was struck by a car which was passing her. Neither driver was hurt, only shaken up. The man, who was driving the other car, helped her out of her car and I helped her to a chair that was in the side yard.

All, she kept saying was how mad her husband was going to be. She kept putting off calling him. She was terrified of him. I offered to make the call, but she said that she had to do it. He would be madder if someone else did. I had called the police as soon as I was sure everyone was accounted for. An officer came and the questions began. I excused myself and went into the house. The husband came. I did go back out then. He didn't make any kind of a scene and they left.

Melinda's case worker informed me of the decision to let Melinda go home for a day on the weekend. I told the case worker that she wasn't ready for this yet. It was a done deal. I told Melinda, she smiled, but her eyes were scared wide open. She wasn't ready for this visit. I called the counselor and she was as horrified as I was at this decision. She called the case worker to give her professional opinion on the subject of the visit, expressing her concern. It didn't matter.

Early on a Saturday morning that Melinda was picked up, I

received a call from her counselor asking me if the visit had been postponed. She was shocked when I told her it hadn't. She asked me to call her on how the visit went. I told her I would.

I taught the children to sort their own dirty clothes and taught them to use the washer and dryer. In the summer, the clothes were hung on an outside clothes line. After they put the clothes in piles— whites, lights, and darks— I would check them to make sure a dark wasn't put in the white or light pile. I found a pair of Melinda's panties with the crotch entirely torn out, hanging by a couple threads. Not a seam coming loose, torn!

I put them in my slacks pocket and asked Melinda to come into my bedroom with me. I showed her the panties, her eyes got big, and she became very nervous. We sat side by side on the bed and I asked her what had happened. She told me she was in the bathroom with the door shut and that she had done that herself. She kept insisting she had done it herself. I couldn't prove, otherwise, but I did put in a call to her case worker. I put in a call to the counselor.

Home visits were suspended for awhile. I still get angry at Social Services attitude of we have to follow the rules...laws. That is primary whether it is a good decision for the child or not. The child is supposed to come first above any of the rest of us involved in the foster child system.

One afternoon, after the girls had come home from school, there was a knock on the kitchen door. It was Melinda's case worker telling me she needed to speak with me. Never would I have come up with the reason why. We sat at the kitchen table with Melinda and Lillian there, too.

I was being questioned on a possible charge of child abuse! The evening before, Melinda was in her bedroom and started yelling and throwing things. I ran upstairs and when I reached for her one of my fingernails slightly scratched her face below her right eye. That was what this was about. She had showed it to her teacher, her teacher sent her to the school nurses' office, the nurse called Social Services, which by law they are supposed to do under suspicious circumstances. I wasn't told what Melinda had told everyone, but it left the nurse with no recourse as to what she had to do.

I couldn't believe this. There could be criminal charges placed against me. I had spent a life time trying not to get in trouble.

I explained to the case worker what had happened. Lillian addressed a question to Melinda, "Why did you tell a lie about grandma for? You know she treats us real good?" Melinda shook her head and smiled.

I was furious and slammed my hand down hard on the table. I said, "My god, you can't please Social Services. I have taken your toughest cases. You told me you give me the toughest cases because you know I can HANDLE it and then you come into my home accusing me of child abuse! Get her out of here!"

The case worker said, "I'm satisfied there was no abuse. There will be no record of this meeting." She left, but not before I told her Melinda could stay. These children have so many problems and having them removed from your home is another rejection. You keep them without resentment for their actions, after you have had a chance to cool down. This was the girl Lillian had tried to drown.

I saw a slow emotional growth in Melinda over time and her school work got better. You could see that with proper nurturing, her life potential could be good. I could envision her future and felt good about it. The decision was made that she was to go back home to live.

My thought was, no, she can't. Isn't there another plan that will allow her to grow into her potential? If she goes home this won't happen. I was heartsick. It all comes back to the fact these are not our children and you know sorrow. It is like a death had occurred.

I have never seen her since or heard anything about how she is doing. I saw her parents and younger sister in a department store. The mother didn't recognize me. The father did. We didn't speak. What was there to say. They were dressed nicer if that could be judged as a good sign. I did.

MAXINE

Her father was black. Her mother was white. They were married. They were divorced. Maxine went to live with relatives. Then she came to me.

She was ten, had short black hair, a little overweight, but solid. Feisty. A nice light tan color to her skin. She was concerned about how people would feel toward her if they knew she was part black, so the first thing she did upon meeting someone new was to tell them. She wouldn't admit she was afraid of being rejected, but I could tell by the look in her eyes and the determined set to her jaw. Get it over with quick was her thinking on the subject. Anger was always below her surface.

There were two girls who lived near by that rode on the same school bus with her. They got to know each other and she would go to their home to play, sometimes. It was fun because the girls had everything they wanted and lax rules. I thought she needed socialization and I had to deal with the fallout.

She went to a church camp for a week. The kids put on a program for the parents. I went and I could tell by Maxine's lack of eye contact with me that something was amiss. I asked her if anything was wrong and she said there wasn't. A girl she became friends with came to me saying she knew something about Maxine that she thought I should know. Maxine was coming on to an older camp counselor.

After the program, I got Maxine aside and asked her about what I had been told. I discussed the consequences of such actions and she agreed it wouldn't happen again. There was only one full day of camp left for which I was grateful.

There is a project that teachers do in their class of young children that I wish they would cease, family genealogy, particularly in these times. I would be so embarrassed whenever this situation would come up in my young life. Most of the kids had their own mom and dad, grandparents, aunts, uncles, cousins, as a daily part of their lives. Holidays, get-togethers, family birthday parties, family reunions. I didn't have that. I sure didn't need to give people any more fodder to look down on me.

This was brought home to me, when it was done in Maxine's class. She was visibly distressed by it. She asked if she could borrow my family. I told her she was living in my home and that made her part of the family. I saw nothing wrong with the idea. I believe, I sent a note to her teacher explaining how it bothered Maxine and such a practice should cease and why. It's tough enough being a foster child, living in someone else's home, without having to prove how screwed up your family is.

One afternoon, Maxine was upstairs in the family room by herself. I heard her talking to herself and the talking kept getting louder until it turned into yelling. I could hear her walking from the front of the house to the back, over and over. The yelling sounded like it was on the brink of rage. I ran up the stairs, two steps at a time, as I believed she might go over the edge emotionally and we might never get her back. Truly. I reached out to get a hold of her. It was like trying to catch a windmill.

I finally got hold of her enough to move the two of us to the couch that was in the room. I managed to get a restraining grip on her, one leg over her closest one to me, holding the right wrist with my left hand, with my right hand in her hair. She was still yelling and fighting like a tiger. She called me every vile name I had ever heard used and some I hadn't.

159

She kept saying for me to get myself off her. Once she started to lower her head toward my arm, then pulled back. A little later she did it again and this time I knew she meant to bite me. I told her, "That would be the biggest mistake of your life," in a serious, calm way. She drew back.

She kept yelling at me to get off her and one time I said what I think was one of the most stupid things I have ever said, "Say you're sorry and I'll let you up." There was no way that child was going to say that. We had been in this position for quite some time. She let out a loud sigh, telling me she had nothing more to say, to which I answered with a thank God, and got up. Her whole attitude changed after this episode. She was much more calm. I think she had stored up so much anger that she couldn't contain it any longer. .

A couple weeks before this event happened she had run away. Lillian came to me, late one afternoon, and said she thought Maxine had run away. I asked her to explain. She thought she had run away. Well, she was looking out an upstairs window and saw Maxine leaving our back yard, walk through the field behind the house, and continue on. I wasn't sure if I was being told the truth or not, so I searched the entire house. Maxine wasn't there.

I told Lillian to get in the car because we were going to look for her. I figured she was too smart to walk on the main road that went by my house, so I headed for a back road. Both roads led to the city where her mother lived. It surprised me when she wasn't on that road. Maybe someone gave her a ride and that thought struck terror in my heart. I crossed over to the main road to go home and call her case worker.

I will be completely honest and say I was getting annoyed with this running away stuff. Foster parents aren't saints. Up ahead, I saw her walking toward us on the opposite side of the road. Annoyance took charge. I sharply pulled onto the shoulder of the road, braking and sending gravel flying back from the car.

I got out, opened the back car door, and looked at Maxine. I saw a look of surprise, then apprehension took over. She continued to walk toward me. I gripped her upper arm and helped her to get into the car. The girls were quiet. I wasn't. I drove around for awhile, so I could calm down. I bought her a baseball cap.

She wasn't done with me yet. I was mowing the lawn, using the riding mower, looked into the kitchen through the double sliding doors as I was driving by when I saw Maxine with the six-inch blade boning knife in her hand. She and Lillian were standing at the end of the kitchen table. I was terrified!

I threw the mower out of gear, walked slowly up the back stairs, praying nothing would happen before I got to them. She looked at me with such a calmness. Slowly, watchfully, I reached for the knife. She gave no resistance.

We had another discussion. Her reason for the action was she wanted to tease Lillian by telling her she was going to cut Lillian's real life like dolls leg off. I thought the talk took. It didn't

Three of my grandchildren were visiting and they all were playing school. My grandson was the principal. I was in the shop working. He came out to the shop and told me that Maxine had used the same knife to threaten him. She did.

I got his side of the story, then I asked her for her side. She asked why should she tell me anything because I'd believe him because he was my grandson. I told her I had already questioned him and that I had called his mother to let her know what had happened. I believe there are two sides to every problem. I don't automatically take one side against the other. That truly seemed to amaze her.

What this action on Maxine's part did do was to make me very afraid to have her around my grandchildren, of which I had many, and the majority were quite young. This fear sent me to the phone in the shop to place a call to her case worker. I explained, I was concerned about my grandchildren's safety. They would have to remove Maxine.

I sat at my desk in the shop for 20 minutes going over and over my decision, in my mind. This would be another rejection for Maxine. I didn't know how she would handle it. We had been getting close.

How do you throw a child away? I made the call to her case worker rescinding my original request. What I was going to have to do was put all the sharp knives and the cooking forks in my bedroom dresser drawer. They were there for four months before I felt it would be safe to put them back in the kitchen drawers.

Maxine had an older sister and three younger siblings. She gave her foster parents a real hard time and ran away all the time. Maxine's brother was in a foster home with the father planning on adopting him. Her two younger siblings, a sister and a brother, had been adopted by a white family. They expressed a desire to the case worker that they would like to adopt Maxine. I met the couple and was favorably impressed by their compassion and desire to give these children a loving and stable home life.

Maxine balked at the idea. She didn't want to move away from her friends. She didn't want to change her last name. I pointed out that when she got married she would be changing her last name. She decided, okay. The visits began.

I was told by Maxine's case worker that she would be removed from my home the very next day after school was closed for the summer. I shot a letter off saying this was totally wrong. Maxine and I had a relationship and we needed time to say a proper goodbye. I asked for five days. I got three.

There was what I called a pavilion in the backyard and summer mornings, bright and early, I would drink my first cup of coffee out there. The children would still be asleep. Peace, quiet, birds singing, sun shining...what a way to start a day.

This one morning, Maxine called out from the kitchen doorway, asking if she could come out and sit with me. I told her she could and to bring her bowl of cereal with her. I told her she didn't have to ask if she could come out to where I was. We had about an hour visit before the rest of the children got up. The next morning she came out with her cereal and we talked some more.

One thing she said to me was, "There was one thing I didn't like here. You were never around." I said, "You mean I was here, but I wasn't here. I was in the shop so much." She replied, "Yes." She left the next morning. She put on a brave front, but I knew her heart. For days, I expected see her, to hear her. I realized I cared deeply for Maxine.

I went to see her twice, once they weren't home. The adopted mother brought her to my home once and to visit some of her friends.

I would like very much to know how she is doing. What is she doing with her life? Is she married? Does she have any children? Is she happy? I was told that as soon as Maxine turned sixteen, she left her adoptive home and moved in with her father and his girlfriend.

This is how you earn your foster parent Purple Heart.

HOLLY

A teenage girl with short dark hair, who habitually ran away from home. She and her mother did not get along.

When I was asked by Social Services to take her into my home, I was told it would only be for a few days, as they were waiting for a bed to open up at an all-girl institution. This was the only recourse left to them because she was past foster home rehabilitation. Her mother had requested Holly not be told she was being moved to the institution because she would run away.

She was pleasant with me and the other children, helpful where she could be. I got the impression she thought she was going to be staying at my home.

I had plans one evening to go to a daughter's home, which was about a 20-minute drive away, to a grandchild's school program. I was taking the foster children with me. I would be gone two hours at the most.

Holly asked if she could meet her boyfriend in the city rather than go with me. I could pick her up on my way home. This presented me with a dilemma. I didn't think it was a good idea, but I also felt I should show I had some trust in her word. This would give her a chance to prove she was reliable.

I agreed, but said I wasn't just dropping her off. I had to meet the boyfriend and I was reserving the right to still say no. He was clean shaven, his hair was clean, his clothes were clean, and what I could see of his body looked clean. They were going to take a walk and would meet me at the nearby school playground.

I got to the playground a little early. It was dark, but there was plenty of street lights so I could see into the play- ground. She wasn't there. I drove around the block a couple times and then pulled up next to the street curb to wait. I was sure she was just late. While I was sitting there, a city police car pulled up across the street from me and asked if I was the lady who was to pick up a young girl by the name of Holly. I told him, I was.

He told me she was at city jail, for me to go straight home, they would bring her there. I did. They did. She had on a pair of large sized boots. She had lost her shoes in a field they had been walking in. She told the police, happily, thank you. They left. She asked if she could take a shower.

Her case worker had called during the day to inform me that she would be at my house the next morning to get Holly. After Holly was done with her shower, I told her we needed to talk. I thought it was unfair for them to use subterfuge on this young girl, as tomorrow they would get her in the car and then tell her where she was going. I thought she needed to be given the chance to prepare herself, emotionally. So, I told her where she was going. She had a look of shock on her face and then, apparently, accepted her fate. I thought, one for the foster kids' side.

The next morning, when she got up, she said she was going to take a shower. I remarked that she had taken one last night. She wanted to be fresh, beings she was leaving. I said, all right. It took awhile for me to notice the shower had been running for, what seemed like, a very long time. I went to the bathroom door and called her name. No answer. I got the tool that would open the door, unlocked the door, and when I looked into the room, the bathroom window was open and she was gone.

I called her case worker, admitting what I had done and that she was gone. I sure botched this case.

It was three weeks before someone turned Holly in as to where she had been hiding out. The sheriffs took her to the institution in the backseat of the patrol car. I had learned a big lesson.

After she was released, she came back to the city. Her name appeared in the local daily paper, frequently, for being in trouble with the law. I am left with the regret. If I had acted as I was told, would this whole thing have turned out differently, for the better?

SASHA AND TONYA

Sasha was five, a little overweight, a real cutie, black, and STUBBORN WITH A DEDICATION. A whirling dervish couldn't outdo her for motion. She had a lot of time outs, accompanied by the reason for the time out.

When I turned my back, she stood up. Constantly. I told her that I could keep up, having her sit back down a lot longer than she could keep standing back up. She must have believed me because, after awhile, this behavior stopped.

She began to behave on her own volition. Problem solved. I've learned that when you have to discipline a child, if you explain the reason for the discipline (the discipline has to fit the degree of the offense) and assure them what will happen if they do it a second time, and follow through with what you said would happen, they get the message.

The right degree of discipline, plus a guaranteed follow through, works wonders. I was told she was sexually molested by her father. He went to jail. Her sister, Tonya, made life miserable for her, while they were in my home.

Tonya was thirteen, reed thin, very tall, pretty, and black. She was more timid around people than Sasha. Whenever she would laugh, she would put her hand in front of the lower part of her face.

The two girls had separate fathers, which had a great deal to do with the meanness she showed toward Sasha. I would notice black marks on Shasha's arms sometimes, as at times there would be four, all in the same area. These were from Tonya pinching her. It had to have hurt, but Sasha never let out a cry, nor did she tell when the action was taking place. I would ask her and even then she was reluctant to tell me her sister had done it. She told me, once, she did it to herself. When I questioned Tonya, she denied doing it, but later when I asked again she admitted she had done it. She didn't know why.

I was at the kitchen sink and looked out the window that was there in time to see Tonya lift Sasha up over her head and body slam her to the ground. I went running out to where they were to check on Sasha.

She was on her feet by the time I got to her. She hadn't been hurt. Tonya and I had a few words. I kept the girls apart. I was concerned what Tonya might do next. I called their case worker and slept upstairs on the couch until their next counselor meeting. I would take the girls to their counselor every week. The counselor would see them separately at times, together and would see me, alone. She saw the hostility.

In New York State, there are stipulations that siblings are not to be separated, but I thought for Sasha's safety that these two sisters should be in separate foster homes. They would still see each other on a regular basis and have the freedom of contact by telephone and letters. Their counselor saw the wisdom of it and agreed with me.

I left her office with the knowledge that the mutual decision would be explained to the girls' case worker. A load had been lifted off my shoulders.

The very first words that were said to me by the counselor on our next visit were that the girls would not be separated. I was stunned by her words. Why didn't the counselor take a stiff stand for her professional belief. This young girl's life was in danger, again. There was no explanation given to me as to why the switch. I have my own theory.

Social Services provided a lot of business for this agency. It is my opinion that was the reason for the switch. I was losing faith in the whole process where foster children were concerned. I called the case worker's supervisor, giving her the facts about Sasha's safety. She told me there is such a law on the books, but some case workers take it too literally and never separate siblings. I noticed she took no action on this issue.

Again, my words concerning what was best for the child were ignored. A foster parent knows these children better than anyone else. We are with them 24/7. Foster homes really are holding centers.

In my area, we are rewarded as foster parents by going free to a local amusement park with food being provided. The children love it and that is great. I'd much rather have them pay attention to what I'm telling them about the children. It doesn't soothe my angst toward Social Services. I know what foster children are feeling. Listen to me.

What fueled Tonya's actions toward Sasha was jealousy. It had to do with Sasha's father, Tonya's stepfather. He told Tonya that he loved her and they had been intimate, then he would spend a lot of time with Sasha. She believed that he loved her. She wanted all his attention. Jealousy is a fiery emotion and I didn't want Sasha around it. I became so disheartened as to my ability to be taken seriously. I could only continue to be a watchdog.

Foster children are used to no structure, doing what they want to, when they want to. McDonald's is their choice of a meal. This led Tonya to tell one of her young woman teachers that she never got to go anywhere. I received a call from the young teacher asking if it would be all right to take Tonya to McDonald's? I told her, she did get to go places and the teacher told me other things that Tonya had told her. She was manipulating the teacher to get what she wanted and it didn't matter if it was a lie. She didn't take her.

I talked to Tonya when she got home from school about this matter. I asked her why she told lies about me? It painted a bad picture of me. Did she know that. Yes. Why? I wanted to go to McDonald's. I wanted attention. This is a constant worry to foster parents, what are the foster children going to say about you. It could get you in a lot of trouble.

Relatives are told to visit their children in the foster parents' home. I was told a large part of the reasoning behind it was they would observe a stable home in action and incorporate some of what they saw into their own homes.

They would be in the living room or kitchen. Usually, they would start in the living room and come to the kitchen if anyone wanted coffee, tea, or cookies. I would be in the next room, out of sight, but not out of hearing range. There could be plans being made for all kinds of activities, possibly talking down the foster parents for their own emotional reasons. The visits were scheduled by Social Services with the foster parents knowing in advance.

I have had some of the children's relatives walking all over my home, looking it over. One lady opened all the kitchen cupboard doors. Another person was going to head upstairs when I stopped her. Some would spend the time talking to me, not their child. I would remind them as to why they were here. At times, no one wanted to talk to anyone.

Transportation was provided for Sasha and Tonya's mother. She lived forty-five minutes away. She kept saying what a pretty house I had. How she liked how I decorated it. What nice things I had sitting on shelves and bookcases. She wished she had a home like it, but she couldn't afford it. She would talk about the girls older brother, who was continually being arrested for stealing. She would bail him out with her welfare money. The last time he got out, he went to a diner and stole $10 from the man sitting next to him. Back in jail.

There was a really good deal on porterhouse steaks, she told me, fifteen $35 dollars. She got a package. Her sons ate all but three in two days. I mentioned to her she should get a large package of ground beef and how many different kind of meals she could get out of it. This wasn't my business, but I was concerned that no one was trying to help her learn how to budget her money. It seemed to me that some Social Services program should be working on this part of her life. I wanted to see her get her act together and to have her daughters back home with her. It would be an uphill battle because she was an alcoholic and used drugs.

Social Services set up for her to attend a drug abuse program. She was to attend all ten meetings. She said she would go. She went to one or two. Then, I heard them tell her if she would go to three she would stand a good chance to get the daughters back home. Didn't go to any. I thought, how dare Social Services tell her she only needed to go to three meetings. No, she needed to go to every damn one! What kind of a lesson of responsibility was that?

The washer and dryer were in the basement of my home. The only way to get to the basement was from the attached garage. I had a light switch put by the kitchen door, so I could turn on the light before I opened the door. One night I was going to do a load of my laundry, opened the kitchen door, then turned on the light. When I turned on the light I heard the back storm door slam shut.

I got frightened and stood listening, hearing nothing more I went to the basement. I got back to the head of the stairs and I heard a motorcycle start up in front of my neighbors house and roar by in the direction the girl's mother comes from when she visits. She had told me he had a motorcycle. Immediately, my mind told me it was the son and he had come to rob me.

I called the case worker the next morning, informing her of what had happened and that I did not want their mother coming to my home again. I didn't want her to give him anymore information about my home. I was told by her that the rules say the parents are to see their children in the foster parent's home. I wrote a letter to the supervisor of the office, located in my area, explaining the situation and that I didn't believe my government would deliberately put my loved ones lives in jeopardy. Some of my grandchildren stayed overnight practically every weekend. I was concerned for their safety.

The meetings were then to be held in the conference room at the Social Services offices. I would take the girls. I never had another such incident in my home. I was grateful for their decision.

The mother and the sisters of the man who was in prison came to visit the girls. They lived about an hour and a half away. It was nice weather. We sat on the deck. She was nice. They were nice. The mother said her son had been wrongly accused and didn't deserve to be in prison. I think that is natural for the most of us. She tried to enlist my support in trying to get him released. No way.

The girls were allowed to go to her mobile home to visit a few times. Their grandmother was told the girls were not to have any contact with her son in any capacity. She let them talk to him on the phone. Sasha told me as she knew this was wrong. She was trying to do what was right. I had to pass this information on to the case worker. No more visits.

What finally happened to the girls was that Tonya was placed in a local home for troubled children. A black foster home had a space become available in their home and Sasha moved there. It was in the same city where her mother lived. I often wonder how the girls are doing and how their mother is doing. I pray they are doing well and are happy.

ALYSHA

Alysha and I met sitting across a table from each other in the kitchen of a group juvenile detention home for children. I had not been asked before to take a child in my home straight from such a situation and I wasn't sure I was up to the challenge. I wanted to meet her face to face and to ask questions. I wanted her to meet me and decide if I was her cup of tea.

Alysha was a little taller than me and a powerfully built girl. I knew if she wanted to she could seriously hurt me. I engaged her in conversation as to her likes and dislikes, her interests. I explained the rules of my home. Fair rules, but to be obeyed rules.

She asked me some questions. I answered them, honestly. Her dark eyes didn't leave my face. Her skin color matched her eyes. We agreed, we would give each other a chance.

The office supervisor and Alysha came on a morning and we went into the living room and sat down. A bombshell was tossed at me. About five miles from my home, Alysha told the supervisor that she thought she was pregnant. What were my feelings about this as to Alysha staying in my home? A lot of thoughts went whirling through my mind and landed on, yes.

The ramifications were settling down in my mind when the next bomb went off. The decision as to how Alysha handled the pregnancy was entirely up to her. I had no say in the making of that decision. None. I could not even discuss it with Alysha.

This didn't set well with me as this was my home, not Social

Services, and I had my own value system way before I became a foster parent. The girl was only a teenager. She needed someone to talk to. IF Alysha needed someone to talk to, Social Services would listen. Good God Almighty, this is a child.

Abortion was mentioned by the supervisor to Alysha as an option. What were my thoughts on the subject if Alysha made such a decision? I told them both I could not emotionally deal with that decision. She would have to leave my home if such a decision was made. In a matter of days, proof came that Alysha wasn't pregnant. I truly was glad Alysha didn't have to make such a huge life, scarring decision at her young age.

The supervisor told me that Alysha wet the bed frequently. I told Alysha that it would be her responsibility to wash her sheets every time this happened, blankets if necessary. There was no sense getting all bent out of shape over it. In time it would cease. Many mornings, Alysha came downstairs carrying her sheets. No words were said. Slowly, it happened less and less.

I was told by the supervisor to take Alysha to the doctors for an internal checkup in preparation to being put on birth control pills. Another thing I didn't believe in. My belief debate went on for quite some time. Do I object, with Alysha's being removed from my home as a result? I finally came to the conclusion that she had been active sexually and would, no doubt, continue to be so. It was best she did not get into an abortion situation again. I took her to the doctors.

Alysha didn't really give me a hard time. I could see it in her eyes, sometimes, that was exactly what she wanted to do. I really saw lightning strike in her eyes once.

It was an evening when we were at an ice cream social at church. She asked if she could go walking downtown with a couple of girls in the small city we were in. My answer was no. That's when lightning struck. I looked back, steadily. She didn't

175

go. That was to her credit.

What she didn't know was that I wanted to be there even less than she did. My demons had broadsided me. I wanted to become a mist so no one could see me. Everyone knew each other. Everyone was talking to each other. Please, don't talk to me. I don't know what to say. I'll say something really stupid and everyone will look at me and mock me.

Only when I'm alone do I feel worthy. No one to compare myself with, then. As soon as I felt we could leave without causing a stir, we did. I could feel Alysha's relief. It mirrored my own.

Alysha went to a weekend church retreat. I felt it would help her in her socialization. Church people are friendly folk, right? The kids were nice to her, but according to the pastor she acted up and would deliberately annoy the other kids. We talked about it a little. It was important for her to have the chance to tell her side. It was pretty much what the pastor said. She didn't feel she fit in. These kids did not have strange men going and coming in their home all the time. They didn't have to sleep on the floor because there wasn't any available bed space.

An "uncle" and his young children came to my home a few times to visit Alysha. He knew her mother. I kept a real close eye on what went on while he was here. I saw nothing out of the way. He seemed genuinely interested in her welfare. I didn't sense any sexual undertones. He lived in a city about forty-five minutes away. I had a swing set in the backyard that no longer got used, so I gave it to him for his children. I had a charcoal barbecue grill that was in good shape. I didn't need that, either.

About now, I could feel myself becoming less and less able to function on a daily basis. I knew I was in trouble emotionally. I had no recourse but to call Social Services and tell them I had to give up being a foster parent. I was having a difficult time taking care of just me. I did my own doctoring. I was suffering from burnout.

I felt sad for Alysha and me. I had grown very fond of her. I wanted her in my home, but it wouldn't be fair to her. She would wind up having to take care of me. She needed to be with people who could handle her natural exuberance and give her direction in her life, preparing her for her adult years. I became lethargic. A grown daughter of mine told me the other day that she could tell Alysha didn't want to leave me.

The day her case worker came to pick her up to take her to a new foster home, Alysha was visibly upset. I could tell she didn't want to leave my home in a car driven by someone else that she hardly knew, to go to a home where she knew no one. I asked if she wanted me to drive her there? Yes, she did. I told the case worker of our decision and I could see an objection coming, and I gave her what my kids call my evil eye, and no objection came forth. It was a quiet ride. I could see tears in her eyes. They matched mine.

They were first-time foster parents where Alysha was going. There were a couple children with the girl being around Alysha's age. It was a black family. People with a higher education will no doubt disagree with me, but I think, if at all possible, a black child should be in a black home. Our cultures are different and that is a good thing.

The three of us got out of the cars and went to the front door. We went inside. I did, too. I was introduced and then I stepped to the sidelines. This was a split level house and I stood at the bottom of the stairs.

In a little while, the case worker came down the stairs, opened the front door and stepped outside. I did, too, but as she walked down the steps, I went back into the house. Just inside. I stood there listening to the conversation, waiting to see how Alysha was going to react to this new family. My plan was to grab her by the hand and take her back to my home if she became hysterical. Subconsciously, I knew I couldn't do that.

There was no outburst and I left. They didn't know I was there. I just wanted to make sure she was all right. Tears cascaded down my face as I drove away. Damn, this is hard.

TWO SISTERS

I was asked to take two sisters. I said, yes. This shows how unable I was to make wise decisions. I had already decided I was not foster parent material anymore and I go and do this. Social Services will keep you on because they didn't have enough foster homes.

These two sisters were around twelve and thirteen. And, they did not want to be in a foster home. They were in one because their father was a gypsy and they have certain customs that are not acceptable in our country. Their mother was Italian.

I showed them to their bedroom and the only time they came out of it was to eat their meals, bathe, and talk to their mother on the telephone.

When their mother would call, she would tell me there was no reason her girls should be in a foster home. She tried to enlist my help in getting them back home. I told her I did not have the power to accomplish what she was requesting.

The younger sister was the brains behind their passive maneuvers, so when one afternoon they came downstairs and asked if they could go outside to the front of the house, red flags went up. The living room door was open.

I heard a car go by and a loud voice saying they would get them away from here. I hurried to where the girls were and got there just before the car made the return trip. An older girl was leaning out the passenger window calling to the sisters as they came near. She saw me and ducked back in the car. They would try again. It was clear that a rescue had been planned.

One more call to Social Services informing the case worker of what had happened and what I was sure would happen again. The girls had only been at my home three days. I told the case worker to remove the girls, immediately. I have never reneged on a responsibility before in my life. I didn't care. I had no inner resources left in which to go the distance one more time. I quit. I just wanted to sit in a rocking chair and slowly move back and forth, period.

The younger sister had told me they didn't like the country. They would agree to being in a foster home, but it would have to be in the city where their parents lived. They were moved farther away to a farm. To me, that was poetic justice. I wasn't even thinking nice thoughts anymore.

All of the children that I have told you about lived in my home within a three-year time period. I haven't forgotten one of them. I have pictures and gifts they handmade for me. They taught me about life, also. Thank you.

CHANGES

Reader's Digest in its April 1993 issue, page 101, had an excellent article on the foster child system's problems written by Trevor Armbrister.

Reader's Digest in its May 1998 issue, page 69, had an excellent article on the foster child system's problems written by Suzanna Chazin.

This is a world wide read magazine that was informing everyone that there was a serious problem with the foster child system years ago, yet nothing has changed.

On March 18, 1994, I mailed a letter to John B. Daly, who was a senator of the 61st district of the State of New York in regard to a foster child situation involving a husband and wife who had been trying to adopt three little sisters that were in their care. The mother agreed to the adoption, then changed her mind, again and again keeping the girls and the foster parents in a constant turmoil. She had not been a mother to the girls in any manner. The little girls wanted to be adopted.

Senator Daly responded to my letter on July 28, 1994. He enclosed a copy of Social Services Law Care and Protection of Children, 384-b, under the heading: Guardian custody of destitute or dependent children; commitment by court order—listed Statement of legislative finding and intent after (a) and (b) are procedures to be followed. They made sense. The problem must be in the rendering of said procedures. I read the entire copy Senator Daly sent me. Did I understand it? You have to be a lawyer. The little girls did get adopted.

I also wrote a letter with recommendation for change in the system to Hillary Clinton when she was residing in the White House. It was shortly after her book *It Takes A Village* was published. I received a letter from the Department of Health & Human Services acknowledging receipt of my letter, directing me to the National Clearing House on Child Abuse and Neglect Information. It had taken all my nerve just to write Mrs. Clinton.

I mailed a letter to Rosie O'Donnell on June 20, 2001, addressed to her magazine about my concern for foster children. She is a highly visible advocate for children's issues. I have not heard anything back from her.

My thought in contacting these people was because of their high visibility and influence in our country. They are people who have the power to press for and achieve change within the foster child system.

In the March 2003 issue of Good Housekeeping, I read an article about Bruce Willis. He said he is working with our current president's administration. He said the system is archaic. He is right. Do I have to write him next?

I have spent many hours concentrating on how to change the current way the foster child system operates. I have sheets and sheets of suggestions but they are basically cosmetic. I do not have knowledge of the entire legality of the system.

I do sincerely believe the current training of people who have expressed a desire to be a foster parent is inadequate, desperately inadequate.

It should be a mandatory requirement that individuals inquiring about becoming foster parents attend meetings, prior to being certified, that explain in DEPTH the legalities involved in becoming a foster parent, the legalities after becoming a foster parent, the reasons children are removed from their birth parents home, how the child/children will react when they arrive at their home, and the degree that reaction can be. The prospective foster parents own children should attend these meetings to help them understand the foster child's situation and learn that these children will not be taking their place in their parents' hearts. These children need a stable, structured, home to live in until their own home situation has improved, allowing them to move back to their parents' home.

There should be professionals at these meetings who can explain about children with damaged emotions and give strategies that have been proven to help. Subjects that should be included are; masturbation, premarital sex, birth control, homosexuality, and pornography. Our world has changed, drastically, over the years.

There should be a child at these meetings who is in the foster child system at this time to tell her/his side of the story from when they entered the foster child system until the point where they are now, telling about their feelings and about the entire experience. At another meeting, there should be someone who is presently a foster parent to share their experiences and answer any questions prospective foster parents want to ask. The answers should not gloss over the problems involved.

This would weed out the faint hearted and the system would have people who are dedicated foster parents. We wouldn't be reading and hearing anymore of those foster parents' horror stories.

Another thing that foster parents must be given is immunity from being sued by the birth parents. A case worker told me of a couple she was interviewing who were thinking of becoming foster parents. She said they were exactly the kind of people that was wanted in the program. The husband asked, would it be all right for a child to mow the lawn as a chore to earn an allowance, to learn responsibility and as a way to blend within the family. The case worker said that would be allowed.

Then the husband asked, if the child got hurt while doing this chore would there be an investigation by Social Services? The answer was yes, and charges could be brought against them if Social Services felt it was negligence. The husband stated he was not willing to take a chance of losing everything he and his wife had worked for to provide for their family and their retirement. A good foster home was lost to deserving foster children.

It should be explained to prospective foster parents that their job is not to save these children. It should be explained that having a foster child in their home is not a "If I don't like the child/children after they have been in my home for awhile, just have them removed." They should be helped to understand that every time a child is removed from one home and shuttled to another, it reinforces to the child that they are worthless and unlovable, damaging their emotions even further. Under such circumstances, the certificate to be a foster parent should be revoked, immediately. These are not items, these are children.

BIRTH PARENTS: I believe they are given too much time to get their life straightened out. Their children are left in limbo, wondering am I staying in the foster home or am I going back home? They can't progress in their life, while their emotions are so turbulent within them. I have met birth parents who are perfectly content to have someone else raise their children and still claim them as "my kids."

After removal of their child/children the birth parent should be given one (1) year to make significant and consistent changes in their life style which can guarantee a safe and caring situation for the child/children to live in. The birth parents rights are secondary to that of the children. During this year, the assigned case worker should make monthly visitations to the birth parents' home to assess progress—if any has been made.

It should be mandatory that birth parents attend classes on parenting skills, personal hygiene, health issues, nutrition, and money management. This should last for six months with access to an additional six months of refreshing on certain areas where there is a problem assimilating the information being provided. Transportation should be provided to these sessions to guarantee attendance. No child should be left in a troubled home while a judge is deciding what should be done with the child/children.

If, at the end of this one (1) year time span there has not been a significant and consistent change in the birth parent's life style, the child/children should be given permanency in a foster home or proceedings began to place the child/children up for adoption. If the birth parents are deemed not able to have their children in their home, yet have good qualities, a program of co-parenting between the foster parents and birth parents should be set up with the child/children remaining in the foster home. It would have been the best possible thing for me if my sister and I had been released to be adopted after our father died. There wouldn't be so many holes in my life and my children would have had a better life.

MY OPINION: There has to be strict structure in helping birth parents to make the necessary changes in their lives for their own positive future, let alone their children's. A lot of birth parents have learned how to work the system to their advantage. They have to learn that won't work any longer. The holding of their hands and the patting of their heads help to give them the attitude of poor me, and the license to continue on as they are. An attitude of why should I try, I get a lot of attention now, and without the thing called responsibility, for my actions. This is not an uncaring attitude of swim or sink. It is providing a life raft to gain control of their life. I have seen this with birth parents that I have been involved with through their children in my home.

DEPARTMENT of SOCIAL SERVICES: The department's primary function should be to remove children from abusive and negligent homes. Then, their responsibility should be one of monitorship of the child's progress while in the foster child system to make the final decision of terminating the birth parents' rights or to return the child/children to the birth parents home. The department duties should be of a legal nature only.

The Department of Social Services, after having given prospective foster parents IN DEPTH TRAINING on their position of being a foster parent, should stay out of the daily lives of the foster home. Decisions that have to be made by the department affecting the child/children with the foster home should be discussed with the foster parents with the final decision made in a manner that will cause the least disruption to the foster home.

Case workers should cease and desist in telling foster children they will receive an allowance at the foster home where they are going, cease telling them that when they are sixteen they can walk away from the foster home to go out on their own, and after a certain amount of days they no longer have to answer to Social Services.

Foster parents, case workers and transporters are the people who take foster children to their appointments that are mainly doctors, dentists and counselors. Case workers and transporters should not stop to buy the children something to eat or buy them an ice cream. It can cause problems in the foster home if there are other children in the home. A foster child needs to feel like any other child in the family and accepted as such.

An example was told to me by a foster mother. They had four children of their own. Their form of discipline was spanking—not a beating, a spanking. They could not spank the foster child because Social Services said this was not allowed. The foster boy became more and more unruly, finally telling the foster parents he didn't think they cared about him. They asked where he got this idea and he told them they didn't spank him when he was naughty like they did the other kids. The spankings stopped.

If a foster child is too disruptive or uncontrollable to be in a foster home the child should be placed in an institution where there are highly trained personnel to work with such children. What SHOULD NOT be done is too keep moving the child from foster home to foster home. They tell themselves, no one wants me, I must be a bad kid, I'm unlovable, and no one will ever want me. Believe me, they do think this way. I did.

No foster child should receive a monthly stipend upon becoming a teenager, without having to work for it. If they do find a summer job or part-time job during the year and quit the job, the stipend should cease. The foster parents' own children do not receive free money when they become a teenager, therefore resentment would be a natural reaction.

I worked at a job for my money and I earned more than money. I learned to have pride in myself as a person, that I wasn't getting a handout, keeping me in a worthless mode because no one thought I would be able to work at a job and succeed.

When people adopt foster children, they receive a monthly check until the child is emancipated. This should not be happening. In the private sector, people who adopt children have to pay for said adoption. Tax payers should not have to pay for someone to adopt foster children. Two of my foster children were in the adoption process when they learned they would receive a monthly check. They accepted it, but wouldn't everyone, really? A good amount of money could be saved if this practice was discontinued.

Meetings between the foster child and their case worker concerning the foster child's feelings toward the foster parent should be discussed somewhere other than the foster parents' home. It puts both parties under an unwarranted level of stress.

The Department of Social Services should not remove a child from a foster home because one of the foster parents becomes ill with a serious illness. Health problems are a fact of life and by removing the child from the home you are teaching the child to run away from problems. We are supposed to guide the child through this sad part of life to become stronger emotionally through our caring support. Disrupting a child's routine has a much more negative result.

My cousin and her husband were foster parents for many years. They adopted a foster child. My cousin developed a heart condition, having angina attacks, which were controlled by medication. Social Services decided to remove the foster children from their home because if she died it wouldn't be good for the foster children to witness.

The children had been with them for quite some time and feelings ran deep on both sides. My cousin called informing me of the children's removal and she was heartbroken. She said it was the first time in forty years that she hadn't put a child on a school bus on the first day of school. The foster children were brought back because they couldn't find another home for them. Everyone was put through this for nothing. My cousin and her husband died in an automobile crash.

The Department of Social Services has a six-month meeting of foster parents, birth parents, counselors, the child's case worker and a Social Services employee who is not involved with this particular child as the child's representative. Sometimes, the child's county appointed lawyer is in attendance. This meeting is to plan the child's next six months. I attended these meetings and it was rare for the children's counselor to be at the meeting. Their opinion has a direct bearing on the child's future, at least it should. It should be mandatory that counselors be at these meetings or lose Social Services as a client. And then enforce it.

The foster child's circumstances are extremely complicated and the need for change is extremely great. Like NOW!

I didn't live life, I programmed it. In the deepest essence of my being it has been a lonely life. I was so focused on the life I wanted for my children that my social skills did not fully develop. I consider myself to be socially challenged. This is my foster child legacy.

My children are caring parents and good citizens. Their children and their children's children are the same. I marvel at how they go out into the social scene with self-confidence and a sense of self-worth. They communicate, they are accepted. This makes everything I have experienced worthwhile. This is also my foster child legacy.

FINIS

EPILOGUE

INVISIBLE PRISON

What is this prison I am in
is it my own doing
or
did others put up these bars
why am I so afraid to be
free
the security of structure will be gone
I'll be exposed to life on its terms
I won't be able to hide behind my facade
can I cover my scaredness with my hands
the anxiety of becoming a lost soul in the crowd
that I won't be a me anymore
feelings of being alone press me like a hot iron
the fear of being in an empty world
these make the bars my companion forever more.

Beverly J. Beach